D0450499

The
Religious Education
of
Older Adults

BETHEL SEMINARY WEST
LIBRARY
4747 College Avenue
San Diego, California 92115

The Religious Education of Older Adults

LINDA JANE VOGEL

Religious Education Press
Birmingham, Alabama

Copyright © 1984 by Linda Jane Vogel
All rights reserved

No part of this publication may be reproduced, stored in a retrieval system, or transmitted, in any form or by any means, elec-
tronic, photocopying, recording, or otherwise, without the prior
written permission of the publisher.

Library of Congress Cataloging in Publication Data

Vogel, Linda Jane.
  The religious education of older adults.

  Includes bibliographical references and index.
  1. Christian education of the aged.   I. Title.
BV1489.V63   1983   268'.434   83-21109
ISBN 0-89135-040-3

Religious Education Press, Inc.
1531 Wellington Road
Birmingham, Alabama 35209
10 9 8 7 6 5 4 3 2

Religious Education Press publishes books exclusively in religious
education and in areas closely related to religious education. It is
committed to enhancing and professionalizing religious education through the publication of serious, significant, and scholarly
works.

PUBLISHER TO THE PROFESSION

TO DWIGHT
with gratitude

Husband, Colleague, Friend
One who enables me to be a lifelong learner

Contents

Tables and Figures

Preface

Writing *Religious Education of Older Adults* has been both challenging and frustrating. I have sought to be informed by a variety of disciplines and fields of study—psychology, sociology, education, theology, and religious education. It is my hope that this book will be helpful to older adults, to persons engaged in planning and implementing teaching-learning opportunities with older persons, and to persons engaged in religious education.

James Michael Lee has been thorough as my editor/publisher. His comments have caused me to rethink many issues and the book is better because of his careful critique.

I am grateful to the following persons who have reviewed my manuscript and who have made helpful suggestions for its improvement: Nelle G. Slater, professor of Christian Education at Christian School of Theology, Indianapolis, Indiana: Arthur C. Burman, professor of Adult Education, The University of Iowa; Robert Herrick, colleague and professor of Sociology at Westmar College; Dwight W. Vogel, professor of Religion and Philosophy, Westmar College; and Joan Phillips, friend and teacher of adults in the church.

I am grateful to my colleagues and friends who serve on the faculty at Westmar College. Their encouragement has helped me persevere when it seemed like there was not time enough to complete this task.

Finally, I am grateful to my husband, Dwight, and to our children, Peter and Kristin, who have been patient and helpful with their wife and mother during the many hours I spent at my office and in the computer center.

It is my prayer that this book will enable persons to grow in love and service to God as they seek to participate in religious education with older adults.

Acknowledgments

Simone de Beauvoir, *The Coming of Age* (New York: G. P. Putnam's Sons, 1972) pp. 131, 276–277, and 807. Permission granted.

Ledford Bischof, *Adult Psychology* (San Francisco: Harper & Row, 1969), p. 224. Permission granted.

Evelyn Eaton Whitehead and James D. Whitehead, *Christian Life Patterns: The Psychological Challenges and Religious Invitations of Adult Life* (Garden City, New York: Doubleday and Company, Inc., 1979) p. 140. Permission granted.

Abraham J. Heschel, "The Older Person and the Family in the Perspective of Jewish Tradition," Carol LeFevre and Perry LeFevre, eds. *Aging and the Human Spirit* (Chicago: Exploration Press, 1981). Not copyrighted material.

Ross Snyder, "In the Aging Years: Spirit," Carol LeFevre and Perry LeFevre, eds. *Aging and the Human Spirit* (Chicago: Exploration Press, 1981) pp. 84–85. Permission granted.

Other copyright permissions to quote may be found in the appropriate chapter notes throughout the book.

CHAPTER ONE

Older Adults and Learning

"It is the meaning that [persons] attribute to their life, it is their entire system of values that defines the meaning and the value of old age. The reverse applies: by the way in which a society behaves towards its old people it uncovers the naked, and often carefully hidden, truth about its real principles and aims" (Simone de Beauvoir, *The Coming of Age*).

Our understanding of persons and the learning process has come a long way. In 1892 William James said that the ideas gained before age twenty-five are the only ideas persons can expect to have![1] By 1928 enlightenment had reached the point where E. L. Thorndike wrote that "nobody under forty-five should restrain himself [herself] from trying to learn anything because of a belief or fear that he [she] is too old to be able to learn it."[2] Eighty years after William James made his assertion, J. R. Kidd proclaimed: "People of all kinds, in all places, and of all ages have a marvelous capacity to learn and grow and enlarge."[3]

Education is not merely a preparation for maturity. Rather, it is "the enterprise of supplying the conditions which insure growth, or adequacy of life, irrespective of age."[4]

Paul Tournier sees education as a process which he be-

1

lieves must continue into old age. He believes "the decisive thing is the desire to learn and the desire to understand, the willingness to undertake something, to try, to persevere, to correct one's mistakes, to strive, to improve, to gain experience and learn the tricks of the trade, to enlarge one's horizon, to broaden one's mind by seeking new paths—at bottom, to grow in love because to be interested is to love, love persons and love things."[5]

Learning can be planned or unplanned. Education, as we are using the term, is planned learning. John Dewey defines education as "the continuous reconstruction of experience."[6] It is an interactive process which leads toward "a more intense, disciplined, and expanding realization of meanings."[7] It is my contention, then, that education is a lifelong process that can enable persons in their becoming.

Education can enable persons in old age to accept themselves as they are, to discover meaning in life as it has been experienced, and to integrate all of life into the person they are. It can aid them in becoming whole.

The Older Adult

When our son was five years old he announced at the table one evening that "thirty is middle age." "Oh, Pete," I said, "what does that make Daddy?" "Three years past middle age!" was his quick reply.

Understanding "old age" (or any age!) is not that simple. We may agree with William Shakespeare's observation in *As You Like It* that old age is when one enters the

"... Last scene of all,
That ends this strange eventful history,
Is second childishness and mere oblivion,
Sans teeth, sans eyes, sans taste, sans everything."

Or we may point to Grandma Moses when we describe old age. She began a career as a painter in her 70s and exuded spirit, creativity, and wisdom. She died at age 101.

Growing old means many things. It means experiencing losses and gaining wisdom; it means slowing down and perhaps seeing life for the first time. Growing old is celebrated and feared; it is accepted and rejected.

The old in American society are more numerous and more visible than ever before. In 1980 there were 25.5 million persons sixty-five and over in the United States; that was 11 percent of the total population.[8] The Census Bureau has projected that 12.2 percent of Americans will be sixty-five and over by the year 2000.[9]

Increased visibility has contributed to a growing concern about problems the elderly face and the need for public policy to deal with issues and problems affecting the old. In fact, a serious study of the aging process in society led Simone de Beauvoir to conclude that once we understand "what the state of the aged really is, we cannot satisfy ourselves with calling for a more generous 'old-age policy,' higher pensions, decent housing, and organized leisure. It is the whole system that is at issue and our claim cannot be otherwise than radical—change life itself."[10]

Within the context of a society that is being forced to confront the needs and problems of a growing number of elderly persons, one finds diametrically opposed stereotypes of what it means to be old. Being old is portrayed as "an autumn, filled with ripe fruit" on the one hand; at the same time, it is pictured as "a barren winter." It is like "the sweet gentleness of a lovely evening" as well as "the dark sadness of twilight."[11] The old may be depicted as "dirty old men" and "crochety old women," or as "wise and witty" and "sensitive and sweet."

Who, then, is the older adult in American Society? Are

any generalizations possible? Can we speak in any meaning-ful way about older adults? Is there any evidence to suggest that old persons will be any better or any worse than the children or middle-aged adults that they once were? Just who is the older adult?

Aging Measured In Years

Perhaps the most commonly accepted way of deciding who is old is to arbitrarily set a chronological age after which one is said to be old. In American society, sixty-five has often been used. Persons became eligible for full Social Security benefits on their sixty-fifth birthday and, until 1978, many persons faced mandatory retirement at that age.

Fifty-five is the birthday which entitles a person to join the American Association of Retired Persons (AARP). Some persons hardly can wait to join AARP and others would be offended if they were given a gift membership.

Since chronological age is an objective fact, it has often been used as a qualifying criterion. Persons can begin school if they were born by a certain date; they can get a driver's license on a certain birthday; they can buy alcoholic beverages after a certain age; and they can run for presi-dent of the United States after they are thirty-five years old. This approach simply has been extended to determine when persons could and should retire.

Chronological age is, in some ways, a fair way of deter-mining when one is seen as too old to work. It treats all persons the same. However, just as all sixteen-year-olds are not equally mature and ready to be responsible drivers, so all sixty-five year olds are not at the end of their occupationally productive years. Chronological age as the only criterion generally does not provide an adequate answer to the question, "Who is the older adult?"

Aging Measured by Function

There is truth in the cliché, "You are only as old as you feel!" Functional age is determined by measuring the way individuals function in given physical, psychological, and social arenas.

In fact, James Birren has pointed out that persons age biologically, psychologically, and socially. Within a given individual, these aging processes occur at different rates. In general, biological maturation is reached first and biological decline begins before persons reach psychological maturity. Persons are slowest to reach social maturity and that is the area which may show little decline in later life.[12]

Biological Aging

Poor health and the fear of poor health are often seen by the elderly as the worst part of being old.[13] That is not surprising when we realize that the body reaches its peak in terms of physical development between age nineteen and age twenty-six.[14]

Even biological aging occurs at different rates in a given individual. All of one's organs do not age at the same rate. The lungs and kidneys age at the same rate; both the lungs and kidneys age at a greater rate than does the heart. We know that the reproductive system ages more rapidly than does the nervous system.

There are many changes in physical appearance that are

associated with aging.[15] The amount of collagen (a protein substance in connective tissue fibers) decreases in the skin as persons age and darkly pigmented spots may begin to appear on the backs of the hands and wrists. Skin breaks easier and heals more slowly as persons age. Wrinkling and sagging occurs. Hair may turn gray or white, and it may even fall out. Hair may grow in men's ears and nostrils and on women's upper lips and chins. Persons may diminish in height and stoop due to the loss of collagen in the spinal vertebrae and/or due to osteoporosis, a condition where bones become less dense and more porous and brittle.

Collagen is also responsible for increasing sluggishness of the heart and for hardening of the arteries. These conditions cause a reduction in the amount of oxygen which is carried to all the vital organs including the brain.

Sensory losses are among some of the more distressing ones for older persons. Vision and hearing decline the most. Loss of hearing often results in persons withdrawing from social interaction and then experiencing loneliness and emotional distress.

For a variety of reasons, old persons move more slowly and with less agility. Reflexes and reaction time slow down.

In spite of these age-related biological changes, it is important to remember that not all persons age at the same rate, and biological dysfunctioning is neither uniform nor universal. In addition, biological aging is clearly related to psychological and sociological factors as well as to environmental factors.

Psychological Aging

Personality is a comprehensive term which refers to the sum total of a person's being that makes that individual unique. By describing personality types, some psychologists have attempted to provide insights into how persons age.[16]

How persons solve problems and adapt is related to psychological aging as is the study of developmental tasks (e.g., Havighurst) and personality development (e.g., Erikson, Peck, and Levinson).

The nervous system, sensory perception, and motor performance are often studied from a psychological perspective. Memory and learning as well as intelligence and creativity may be included as persons study aging from this perspective.[17] Self-image, the way one sees oneself and one's relationship to others, is a key concept when studying older adults and the aging process. Many of these topics will be explored in later chapters.

Sociological Aging

Social gerontologists spend a good deal of time studying changing roles in the latter stages of life. Roles are interactional. At the same time, any given individual will have multiple roles which may call for conflicting loyalties or actions.

Role differentiation and adult socialization become less focused as persons grow old in society.[18] Work roles, familial roles, and community roles are likely to be altered or lost at a period in life when social norms are so uncertain that some sociologists describe being old as a "roleless role."[19]

The sociological study of aging focuses on persons interacting in a social context. It examines social institutions and their impact on persons. In this book we will examine educational and religious institutions and how they affect and are influenced by older adults.

Functional age has been used by some researchers in an

effort to determine, more accurately than chronological age can, the performance level of persons. Functional age is established by using ability tests in order to determine a person's level of functioning in physical, psychological, and social arenas. This, many claim, is much more useful than knowing how many birthdays an individual has celebrated.[20]

Aging Viewed As Stages

Another way of dealing with age is to examine it by studying developmental stages in the adult life cycle. Much is currently being written about the adult life cycle and its stages or seasons. This approach merits careful scrutiny.

Robert Atchley suggests that age can be seen in stages by linking young adulthood, middle age, later maturity, and old age to sets of physical, psychological, and social characteristics that typify each stage in life.[21]

Characteristics which depict a given stage generally do not include chronological age. For example, later maturity may be characterized by some physical decline, less available energy, and an increase in chronic conditions as well as by retirement. Old age is generally characterized by physical frailty, a breakdown in one's social networks, and more concern with the past than the future. Chronological age ranges may then be used to describe groups that tend to exhibit these traits. Neugarten has suggested that there is a need to further refine the stage, old age, into the "young-old" (fifty-five–seventy-five) and the "old–old" (seventy-five plus).[22]

It becomes abundantly clear as we study the aging process and old age that it is a gross over-simplification to try to speak meaningfully about the broad category, "old age." It allows no more precision than we have when we speak about "childhood." Developmental psychologists now recognize that we can say very little about "the old"; it has become necessary to make distinctions between the young old and the frail old. Health and social roles may be much more significant than chronological age in understanding persons in the latter third of life.

Social roles may play a major part in describing and defining a given stage in the adult life cycle. For example, the time when the last child leaves a parental home (often referred to as the "empty nest") can easily occur from the time some parents are nearing forty through the time when other parents reach their seventies. The loss of the active, day-to-day parent role may become a significant factor for aging persons regardless of their chronological age.

Aging: A Holistic View

In understanding aging, one must take into account the interrelatedness of chronological age (years lived), social time (which is determined by age norms and how persons interact with the environment), and historical time (involving particular events like a war, recession, teachers' strike, etc.).[23] One must also be cognizant of both cognitive and affective factors. Beliefs, values, and lifestyle must be considered if one is to view aging persons holistically.

The study of aging (gerontology) has generally been seen as an interdisciplinary field of study that includes biological, psychological, and sociological aspects of aging. Any attempt to understand the aging process and aged persons must examine these areas and the ways in which they interrelate. A holistic approach is based on the belief that the reality of aging and old age is more than just the summation of biological, psychological, and sociological data. However, how all these data interface and interact create the reality that we call aging.

Ponce de Leon is illustrative of the desire persons have to seek the fountain of youth; throughout history persons seem to seek a way to stop the aging process in the human body. The first aging research that was done tended to focus on biological aging, and many theories have been proposed.[24] For example, a variety of theories examine the role that genetics, the immune system, molecular functioning, the endocrine system, and the nervous system play in the aging process. Certainly, biological aging is one aspect that must be considered when we try to understand the older adult.

Psychological aging is an umbrella term that has generally been used to encompass sensory and psychomotor processes, the ways in which persons perceive, what drives and motivates them, their emotions and their mental capabilities. Studies in this area may focus on any psychological changes in humans that may be age-related.

None of these biological and psychological age-related changes occur in a vacuum. Persons are affected by their environment, and these changes influence the individual's ability to function in a social setting. Therefore, to really understand older persons, one must seek to understand the sociological aspects of aging as well. In addition, historical events affect each other and are factors which impinge upon and make an impact on the aging process.

These considerations are related to what psychological literature refers to as the maturing process. Harry Overstreet points out that mature persons have not attained a certain point on an achievement scale; rather, their linkages with life are always in the process of becoming stronger and richer as their attitudes develop and encourage their growth.[25]

Maturing is a lifelong process. Persons move along continua as they mature. Leon McKenzie points out that many different areas need to be considered as one examines the life continuum. Economic independence, biological maturity, societal expectations and rites of passage, and educational achievement all play a part in defining when one is adult.[26] Malcolm Knowles suggests continua such as these for measuring maturity: from dependence to autonomy; from narrow interests to broad interests; from an amorphous self-identity to an integrated self-identity; from imitation to originality; and from impulsiveness to rationality.[27]

Accepting these ideas about maturation will have important ramifications for the purposes and practices of adult religious education as well as for our understanding of how older adults learn.

Since older adults are viewed as moving toward self-directedness and self-responsibility, it is reasonable to assume that they will determine, or should be enabled to determine, the purposes for any education they choose to undertake. Cyril Houle suggests that adults engage in learning activities from three basic orientations: learning for learning's sake, an activity orientation, or a goal orientation.

What has been said about maturing refers to all adults—young, middle-aged, and old. In fact, some older adults may be expected to be farther along on the maturity continuum than those younger in years. Older adults may be expected to be dealing with issues revolving around Erik Erikson's generativity and/or integrity issues. They may have to cope with sensory losses and an increase in chronic illnesses. They may also be faced with losses of economic or physical independence. Nevertheless, older adults have a richness of lived life to bring to each new day.

The continuity theory[28] claims that there are no dramatic or abrupt changes brought on by aging. Rather, individuals approach change and cope with aging using processes and approaches that they have developed throughout their lives. Bernice Neugarten claims that it is possible to successfully predict the aging patterns of individuals if we know their personality in middle age and how they have dealt with earlier events in life.[29] This sense of continuity provides the foundation for examining a developmental approach to aging.

Currently, much is being written about adult development and the adult life cycle. Terms like "marker events," "crises," "stages," and "developmental tasks" are being widely—and sometimes imprecisely—used. Whichever terms one uses, it is important to remember that they are descriptive of a large number of persons in our culture but that they should not be viewed as prescriptive for any particular individual. It seems important to examine and define the terms we use (see glossary) in order to construct a holistic, developmental approach which can aid us in understanding older adults.

"Life phases" is a term that may be more helpful than "stages" even though they are often used interchangably. Stages may imply sharper lines than really exist. "Life phases" is a term we will use to describe periods in the older adult life cycle that seem to evolve because of developmental tasks or marker events that many persons experience within a particular chronological time span.

Bernice Neugarten has written extensively on the life

course. She uses terms like "social time" and "cultural clocks" to describe the "age organization of society as a dynamic, socially meaningful, and psychologically meaningful system." She observes, however, that persons' lives can be appropriate when their internal clocks are not synchronized with our society's cultural clocks. There is some evidence to suggest that we are, in fact, moving toward a more age-irrelevant society where more variance in "social time" is being fostered or at least tolerated.[30] Even so, concepts like social time and cultural clocks can contribute to our understanding of life phases.

Understanding and describing the cultural clocks that emerge when one studies large numbers of persons is helpful so long as we remain clear that the life phases we have identified are descriptors; they must not be viewed as norms. This warning is made even more crucial because some of the best studies on stages or phases of the adult life cycle have gathered much of their data from white males.[31]

A psychosocial approach to human development is one that focuses on the interactions between the individual's biological traits and personality, and the environmental and social realities which are a part of that person's world. While recognizing individual differences, it is believed to be possible to describe developmental tasks that can be associated with various phases of the life cycle.

A structural developmental approach focuses more on cognitive development and is less concerned with the sociological aspects of human development. Whether one takes a psychosocial[32] or a structural developmental[33] approach to the study of the adult life cycle, self-identity seems to be a key to periods of transition. Our approach will be psychosocial.

Change may be a sign of life and growth. Change is a

present reality in the lives of persons. Like persons, change comes in a variety of forms. Changes in persons' lives may be the substitution of one attitude or practice for another. Much of the change persons experience is simple, incremental (gradual) change. It may be imperceptible. There eventually comes a time when cumulative changes within an individual create a reality that can be helpfully described by a different life phase. On the other hand, change that is tumultuous can be brought on by a crisis. Whatever its form, change can be growth producing.[34]

Crises in the adult life cycle may be "on schedule" as Bernice Neugarten indicates when she writes of "social clocks"; they may be "misscheduled" by being either premature or delayed; and they may be "overscheduled" which can lead to self-fulfilling prophecy. Evelyn and James Whitehead maintain that those crises that are unexpected and "off schedule" are likely to be the most difficult to handle.[35] Movement from one life phase to another may be triggered by a crisis.

Transitions arise when one's life structure is no longer adequate to deal with life and persons find themselves moving toward a different life structure that will more adequately meet their needs. Daniel Levinson [36] maintains that no life structure is permanent and that stabilization is a temporary status that rarely lasts more than ten years.

As persons continue to grow and mature, they do move through periods of transition. Key questions in any transition period seem to revolve around basic issues like these: Who am I? How can I be a contributing member of society? How can I assume responsibility for and feel good about the choices I make? These are questions that persons in the last third of the adult life cycle continue to struggle with as they grow older.

Douglas Kimmel[37] uses the term "milestones" to refer to events like the death of one's parents, menopause, children leaving home, grandparenthood, retirement, and death of spouse. "Marker events" is the term Gail Sheehy [38] uses to refer to concrete events like these. She points out that movement from one developmental phase to another may or may not be triggered by marker events. Developmental phases are more basic—they involve an inherent unfolding of the personality that can be viewed as a sequential, predictable process.

Erik Erikson is well known for having divided the life cycle into eight stages of self development.[39] However, Erikson focused more on the first half of life than on the latter half. Only three of his eight stages focus on adulthood. For him, early adulthood is the time when persons must develop the ability to deal with intimacy if they are to avoid isolation. Midlife is the time when they must face the issue of generativity or experience self-absorption. Finally, in old age, persons resolve the issue of integrity, or they fall victim to disgust and despair.

Robert Peck[40] expanded on Erik Erikson's schema for the latter half of life. He subdivided Erikson's final stage, integrity vs. disgust, into three categories. When persons face retirement they are forced to come to terms with the issue of ego-differentiation vs. work-role preoccupation. As persons' physical health begins to decline, they must deal with the issue of body-transcendence vs. body-preoccupation. Finally, when persons accept the fact that they will die, they must confront the issue of ego-transcendence vs. ego-preoccupation. It seems clear that these issues which Peck describes relate directly to the questions of self-identity which we have suggested are a part of every transition period.

Howard McClusky suggests a hierarchy which may elaborate on or parallel Erik Erikson's final stage—ego-integrity vs. despair. McClusky's work clearly correlates with Abraham Maslow's hierarchy and Robert Peck's elaboration of Erikson, as well.

Howard McClusky says that persons must first satisfy their *coping needs.* Included here are physical and economic needs as well as educational needs. Once these are met, persons must respond to their *expressive needs.* This involves sharing what one is and has with others. Then come *contributive needs.* Persons need to give and to be needed. Once these needs are met, persons have *influence needs* which relate to impacting the environment and the larger society. Finally, persons, particularly in old age, must face the *need for transcendence* as they seek to make meaning of life and death.[41]

Roger Gould[42] has observed that sometime after age fifty adults are able to review their life and to make contact with what he calls their inner core. It is only at this point that individuals may achieve an inner directedness that enables them to accept themselves as who they are. They are able to say "yes" to who they are and to be secure about their self-concept. They can then center the rest of their life around their own uniqueness because they will have discovered that human worth resides within.

Those who fail to make this discovery, Gould maintains, will continue to cling to power and status as measures of their worth and will be plagued with envy, jealousy, and, finally, meaninglessness. Again, this suggests a return to the self-identity questions we proposed.

Evelyn and James Whitehead build on the work of Erik Erikson and Robert Havighurst to develop this idea of the inner strength that may come with mature age. They believe that movement into this period of personality expansion becomes possible in late adulthood when persons reflect on and evaluate their life as meaningful or absurd. Growth toward human maturity is enabled when one's life is judged by one's self to be more an expression of "wholeness and affirmation" than of "negation and despair."[43]

An eighteenth-century playwright, Pierre Beaumarchais, may have been reflecting this reality when he wrote: "Oh, my children! There comes an age when right-thinking people forgive themselves for their errors and former weaknesses, and so behave that a gentle, affectionate attachment takes the place of the stormy passions that once divided them."[44]

David Moberg has studied personal adjustment of older adults and has given special attention to spiritual well-being and to the role church membership may play. Moberg identifies a number of issues which are related to the spiritual well-being of older adults. These include needs arising from sociocultural sources, a working through of anxieties and fears, coming to terms with death, achieving a sense of integration in one's life, accepting that one is of worth, and finding congruence through one's own philosophy of life.[45]

Spiritual well-being has been defined as "the affirmation of life in a relationship with God, self, community, and environment that nurtures and celebrates wholeness."[46] It is something persons can grow toward as they engage in becoming.

Daniel Levinson[47] writes that an integrated life structure necessitates a "goodness of fit" between one's lived roles and one's inner self. This means that one must establish equilibrium between one's way of being in the world and one's self-understanding.

Older adults, then, can expect to pass milestones—to experience marker events. There are gains. For example, persons might experience fewer demands from family, increased leisure after retirement, or opportunity to pursue deferred life goals. They may experience a sense of peace from increased maturity, a broader perspective, and greater sensitivity. There are also losses. For instance, many older adults face financial difficulties or grieve from loss of the work role, loss of status, loss of health, or loss of spouse.

Older adults are impelled to review their life's accomplishments and to come to terms with the worth and meaning which their life has. They may be ready to struggle in a deep and profound way with questions of self-identity and the meaning of life.

It is also true that once older adults have made the transition into old age and have developed a life structure that fits them where they are, they may not want to struggle with questions of worth and value and meaning. Their needs and wants will differ greatly from those who have not yet resolved the developmental issues which Erikson and Peck describe.

Summary

Older adults come in all sizes, shapes, and personality types. They reflect the historical periods and the social situations out of which they come. Each one has a biological, psychological, and sociological autobiography which has contributed to the unique person each individual has become and is becoming.

As we develop a holistic understanding of the older adult, we must seek to understand the relationships among the various aspects of aging—the biological, psychological, and sociological—as well as the role historical events and personal autobiographical events play. It is my contention that a developmental approach must inform the conceptual framework of a holistic approach to understanding the older adult and the aging process.

The older adult, then, can be described as in the last third of the life cycle. There are certain milestones or marker events which they might be expected to have experienced. There are developmental issues with which they must yet deal.

It seems likely that older adults must confront issues relating to assuming an inner-directedness for who they are and for growth toward spiritual well-being. They must face issues revolving around questions of integrity and transcendence.

Finally, each older adult is a unique person of worth who has succeeded to a greater or lesser degree in living life with meaning. The task we face is to explore the needs for and opportunities inherent in religious education with older adults.

Chapter One Notes

1. William James, *Psychology* (New York: Henry Hold & Co., 1892).
2. E. L. Thorndike, *Adult Learning* (New York: Macmillan, 1928).
3. J. R. Kidd, *How Adults Learn*, rev. ed. (New York: Association Press, 1973), p. 7.
4. John Dewey, *Democracy and Education* (New York: Macmillan, 1916), p. 61.
5. Paul Tournier, *Learn to Grow Old* (New York: Harper & Row, 1972), p. 113.
6. Dewey, *Democracy and Education*, p. 93.
7. Ibid., p. 417.

8. Jacob S. Siegel and Cynthia M. Taeuber (U.S. Bureau of the Census). "The 1980 Census and the Elderly: New Data Available to Planners and Practitioners" (Unpublished paper, October, 1981), p. 1.

9. Robert C. Atchley, *The Social Forces in Later Life: An Introduction to Social Gerontology*, 3rd ed. (Belmont, California: Wadsworth Publishing Company, 1980), p. 9.

10. Simone de Beauvoir. *The Coming of Age* (New York: Warner Paperback Library, 1970), p. 807.

11. Ibid., p. 314.

12. J. E. Birren, *The Psychology of Aging* (Englewood Cliffs, New Jersey: Prentice-Hall, 1964).

13. Richard A. Kalish, ed., *The Later Years: Social Applications of Gerontology* (Monterey, California: Brooks/Cole Publishing Company, 1977), pp. 158–159.

14. Jeffrey S. Turner and Donald B. Helms, *Contemporary Adulthood,* 2nd ed. (New York: Holt, Rinehart and Winston, 1982), pp. 28–31.

15. For a discussion of physical aging, see Lewis R. Aiken, *Later Life,* 2nd ed. (New York: Holt, Rinehart and Winston, 1982), pp. 28–51.

16. See S. Reichard, F. Livson, and P. G. Petersen. *Aging and Personality* (New York: John Wiley, 1962). They describe five personality types of retired men as follows: mature, rocking-chair, armored, angry, and self-haters. Personality types are correlated with role behavior in order to study successful adaptation to aging.

17. Kalish, *The Later Years,* pp. 47–57.

18. Irving Rosow, *Socialization to Old Age* (Berkeley: University of California Press, 1974).

19. For a more extensive discussion of a social view of aging see Kalish, *The Later Years,* pp. 62–77.

20. For a brief discussion of functional age, see James E. Birren and V. Jayne Renner's article in the *Handbook of the Psychology of Aging,* ed. J. E. Birren and K. Warner Schaie (New York: Van Nostrand Reinhold, 1977), pp. 15–17.

21. Atchley, *The Social Forces in Later Life,* p. 7.

22. Bernice L. Neugarten, "Age Groups in American Society and the Rise of the Young Old," *Annals of the American Academy of Political and Social Science* (September, 1974), pp. 187–198.

23. Bernice L. Neugarten, "Personality and Aging," in *Handbook of the Psychology of Aging,* pp. 626–649.

24. See an introductory textbook on social gerontology. For example, see Robert C. Atchley, *The Social Forces in Later Life* (3rd ed.), 1980; Beth B. Hess and Elizabeth W. Markson, *Aging and Old Age,* 1980; Arthur N. Schwartz and James A. Peterson, *Introduction to Gerontology,* 1979. Or see

Nathan W. Shock's article, "Biological Theories of Aging," in Birren and Schaie's *Handbook of the Psychology of Aging*, pp. 103–115.

25. Harry A. Overstreet, *The Mature Mind* (New York: W. W. Norton, 1949), p. 43. It is important to distinguish our understanding of maturing from maturational which refers to the biological processes of aging.

26. Leon McKenzie, *The Religious Education of Adults* (Birmingham, Alabama: Religious Education Press, 1982), pp. 116–121.

27. Malcolm Knowles, *The Modern Practice of Adult Education: Androgogy Versus Pedagogy* (New York: Association Press, 1970), p. 25.

28. Robert Atchley (1980) maintains that the continuity approach to understanding how persons age is based on the belief that "in the process of becoming adults, individuals develop habits, commitments, preferences, and a host of other dispositions that become a part of their personalities. As individuals grow older, they are predisposed toward maintaining continuity" (p. 27). Also see Lewis R. Aiken, *Later Life,* 2nd ed. (New York: Holt, Rinehart and Winston, 1982), pp. 102–109.

29. Bernice L. Neugarten, "Grow Old Along With Me! The Best Is Yet to Be," in Moss and Moss, eds., *Growing Old,* p. 112.

30. See Bernice L. Neugarten and Gunhild O. Hagestad, "Age and the Life Course" in the *Handbook of Aging and the Social Sciences,* ed. Robert H. Binstock and Ethel Shanas, pp. 35–55. Also see Bernice Neugarten interviewed by Elizabeth Hall, "Acting One's Age: New Rules for Old," in *Psychology Today,* April, 1980.

31. Note, for example, that Daniel Levinson's study reported in *The Seasons of a Man's Life* is based on extensive data gathered from forty males, five of whom were black. Levinson's study is carefully done and his procedures and samples are clearly defined. He is now working on a study involving women subjects. Nevertheless, the preface of his current book begins "What does it mean to be an adult?" His title is clear—except that many persons still consider "man" a generic term. Others, less precise than Levinson, have made generalizations based on Levinson's study about the "adult life cycle."

32. Persons often associated with a psychosocial perspective include Freud, Jung, Havighurst, Erikson, Levinson, Sheehy, Neugarten, Valliant, and Gould. The psychosocial approach examines self-image, roles, and relationships as they affect and are affected by the aging process. Life phases, seasons or stages, and developmental tasks are seen as descriptors of predictable periods in the life cycle.

33. Persons often associated with a constructive developmental approach which focuses on epistemological questions include Kant, Hegel, Dewey, Piaget, and Kohlberg. A constructive developmental approach examines *how* persons know and value rather than *what* persons know or

do. The developmental stages in this approach refer to the patterns and processes persons use to organize what they know and value. An excellent discussion comparing the psychosocial approach and the constructive developmental approach can be found in James Fowler's essay in *Faith Development in the Adult Life Cycle,* Kenneth Stokes, ed. (New York: Sadlier, 1982), pp. 178–207.

34. Evelyn Eaton Whitehead and James D. Whitehead, *Christian Life Patterns: The Psychological Challenges and Religious Invitations of Adult Life* (Garden City, New York: Doubleday, 1979), p. 49.

35. Ibid., p. 51.

36. Daniel J. Levinson, *The Seasons of a Man's Life* (New York: Random House, 1978).

37. Douglas C. Kimmel, *Adulthood and Aging* (New York: John Wiley & Sons, Inc., 1974).

38. Gail Sheehy, *Passages: Predictable Crises of Adult Life* (New York: E. P. Dutton & Co., Inc., 1974).

39. Erik Erikson, *Childhood and Society* (New York: Norton, 1950).

40. Robert C. Peck, "Psychological Developments in the Second Half of Life" in Bernice Neugarten, ed., *Middle Age and Aging* (Chicago: The University of Chicago Press, 1968), pp. 88–92.

41. Howard Y. McClusky, "Education for Aging: The Scope of the Field and Perspectives for the Future" in Stanley Grabowski and W. Dean Mason, eds., *Learning for Aging* (Washington, D.C.: Adult Education Association of the U.S.A., 1976), pp. 324–355.

42. Roger L. Gould, *Transformations: Experiencing Growth and Change in Adult Life* (New York: Simon and Schuster, 1978).

43. Whitehead and Whitehead, *Christian Life Patterns,* p. 160.

44. Quoted by Simone de Beauvoir in *The Coming of Age,* pp. 276–277.

45. David O. Moberg, "Spiritual Well-Being: Background and Issues for the Technical Committee on Spiritual Well-Being," *1971 White House Conference on Aging* (Washington, D.C.: Government Printing Office, 1971).

46. NICA, *Spiritual Well-Being—A Definition* (Athens, Georgia: National Interfaith Coalition on Aging, 1975).

47. Levinson, *The Seasons of a Man's Life.*

CHAPTER TWO

Education and the Older Adult

"And not the body alone must be sustained, but the powers of the mind much more; unless you supply them, as oil to a lamp, they too grow dim with age" (Cicero, in "On Old Age").

A Brief History

Early Period

Documents from the very beginning of the development of this nation indicate that it was founded on two educational ideals prized by the Puritans: "a learned clergy and a lettered people."[1] One of the early concerns of the colonists was to provide basic education for the children of the colonies.[2] Religion and the ability to read Scripture were integrally related to education in this period. Any adult education that may have taken place during the colonial period was "essentially unorganized and primarily vocational."[3]

The birth and growth of these United States were more egalitarian than the European countries from which many of our ancestors came. That meant that ways had to be found to inform and educate the populace. Newspapers became important—reportedly 366 were being published in 1810. The lyceum movement which fostered local study groups flourished. In 1831, for example, 1,000 towns sent representatives to an organizational meeting for the National American Lyceum. Public libraries were developed—especially in urban areas. Free town libraries appeared on the scene in 1833 and the Boston Public Library opened in 1852.[4] Evening schools for workers were established throughout the nineteenth century, but these generally served the needs of teenagers who worked during the day. In 1862, with the passage of the Morill Land Grant Act, the groundwork that would encourage agricultural education for rural adults was laid.

The church has been seen as the "single most universal instrument for intellectual activity" during the colonial period and probably for the first two hundred years of American History. In addition to scholarly and intellectually rigorous preaching, colonial churches sponsored midweek services and lectures.[5]

The Sunday School movement begun by Robert Raikes in Gloucester, England, in 1780, provided a model that was quickly picked up in Colonial America. The Methodist Conference in Charleston, South Carolina, officially recognized Sunday Schools in 1790.

While the Sunday School's primary goal was "to bring every child and youth . . . under the influence of the gospel," the movement took Sunday School libraries everywhere it went.[6] Paul Vieth asserts that the Sunday School Union was committed to reaching the masses *of all ages*. Indeed, already in 1817 the Philadelphia Sunday and Adult School Union had been formed. This was the forerunner of the Sunday School Union which was formed in 1824 and had its headquarters in Philadelphia. The Sunday School became a ready-made vehicle for Christian teaching and learning that involved adults, as teachers and as learners, as the spirit of the Second Great Awakening spread across America.[7]

The American Sunday School Union, begun in 1824, adopted a resolution in 1828 which asserted that the Sunday School was "eminently adapted to promote the intellectual and moral culture of the nation . . . and to reconcile eminent national prosperity with moral purity and future blessedness."[8]

By the time of the Civil War, it was a generally accepted belief that children and youth must be educated in both basic and religious education in order for a free and democratic nation to develop. The idea that adults could continue learning had been planted and would soon blossom.

Post-Civil War America

Following the Civil War there was great impetus toward technological and scientific education. Reform was underway as the old ways following the pattern of the English universities were judged to be inadequate. Technical, practical, and democratic ideals were espoused.

Science provided the tools for reform; the land grant colleges served as a primary institution where the reform could be carried on. There were great struggles as these land grant colleges developed into viable institutions. Struggles arose involving those who were committed to the classical-bound traditions of higher education and those who wanted all practical, mechanical arts. The Grange, whose members believed that land grant colleges were a means to enable farmers' sons to escape the farm, legislators who were expected to please both urban and rural constituents, those who asserted that liberal arts standards had to be upheld, and those who were committed to making higher education available to all without regard to background or ability struggled to find allies who would support their points of view.

In spite of many conflicting views, by the turn of the century, vocational and technical education had evolved to become an integral component of American higher education.[9] In this way the possibility that education could be for adults as well as children and youth was enhanced.

Immigration, industralization, and urbanization provided unique challenges to individuals and for the society as a whole. One response to a felt need for learning was the Chautauqua movement, begun in 1874.

Chautauqua[10] was conceived by two Methodists—John H. Vincent, who later became a bishop; and Lewis Miller, who was raised on a farm and become an inventor and manufacturer. These co-founders began by planning for the Fair Point Sunday School Assembly in order to provide training for Sunday School teachers who often lacked formal education in Scripture study as well as in pedagogy.

The immediate success of the Chautauqua movement might be attributed to a variety of factors—an idyllic setting, a time when people were hungry for learning, extensive publicity, the use of well-known and dynamic speakers, the commitment to provide free or low-cost printed resources to persons across the land, and the development after the fifth Chautauqua Assembly in 1878 of Chautauqua Literary and Scientific Circles (C.L.S.C.) throughout America. These circles, involving 100,000 persons by 1888, provided an opportunity for self-education to persons on the frontier as well as in more settled communities.

The C.L.S.C. members were soon eager for "little" Chautauquas where they lived, and by 1890 there were almost two hundred such "independents." What began in New York in 1874 blossomed into a grassroots movement which fostered learning and intellectual debate among both the educated and the uneducated who were becoming educated through Chautauqua. Its initial focus—to train Sunday School teachers—was broadened to include religion, education, and the arts. Chautauqua was an idea whose time had come and its impact on persons and churches was immeasurable.

Even though the Sunday School was founded for persons of common-school age, it had been greatly enhanced by the Chautauqua movement and had become an important institution of learning for persons of all ages. By 1872, when the Uniform Lesson system was adopted, materials were being provided for persons of all ages from four-year-old children through adulthood.[11]

The Twentieth Century

Chautauqua was initiated to train Sunday School teachers, as we have seen. However, it quickly developed a much broader base. Chautauqua has been held every summer since it was founded in 1874 at Lake Chautauqua, New York. Chautauqua has developed into a much broader form of adult education where thousands gather to be renewed through the arts and through religious and philosophical lectures and classes.[12] Three orchestras were in residence during a recent summer. Discussions were held on abortion, a lecture was given by the president of the National Council of Churches, and a course was offered on "Battling Burn-Out." So it is that Chautauqua remains a significant adult education institution today. In the course of its development, Chautauqua is credited with a variety of

new educational forms and methods including "correspon-
dence study, summer school, university extension, and
book clubs."[13] It has also provided an important model for
leadership training for religious educators.

By 1920 the extension service had grown tremendously.
It had shown that adult education could make a positive
and significant contribution to the lives of rural Americans.

Evening schools which had had a tenuous beginning now
experienced growth in scope and in the number and age of
participants. The curriculum was broadened at the beginning of the twentieth century in four areas: "1) expansion
of "Americanization" programs for immigrants; 2) expansion of vocational courses . . . ; 3) extension into secondary
and college level subjects . . . ; and 4) experimental sorties
into informal adult education."[14]

Several historical events had real impact on the educational development of persons in this century. World War I
cut short the education of many males. Then the great
depression influenced the direction of the lives of those
persons who were in their teens in the 1930s. Many of them
were deprived of the opportunity to complete high school
or to go to college. The G.I. bill following World War II and
the Korean conflict provided the opportunity for returning
veterans who were older than the typical college student to
continue their education in colleges and universities.

Education has been seen as a positive value in our society.
This is illustrated by the fact that the number of years persons have attended school has continued to increase during
this century (see Table 2.1).

Other data show that in 1970, 40.4 percent of the population aged 55–64 were high school graduates while only 24.1
percent of those 75+ had graduated from high school. The

Table 2.1[15]

Sex and year	Median school years completed		Percentage of high school graduates	
	65 years old and over	25 years old and over	65 years old and over	25 years old and over
Both sexes				
1965	8.5	11.8	23.5%	49.0%
1970	8.7	12.2	28.3	55.2
1975	9.0	12.3	35.2	62.6
1980	9.7	12.4	37.9	65.4

Source: Adapted from U.S. Bureau of the Census, *Current Population Reports*, Special Studies Series P-23, No. 59, U.S. Government Printing Office, Washington, D.C., 1976, p. 50.

difference in amount of education between old and young, however, can be expected to decrease in the future.[16]

Adult Education Today

A number of factors have contributed to the growing view that education is a basic right of all persons in every age group.[17] Persons of all ages and stations in life are returning to education to claim what they missed "when they were of 'school age.'"[18]

The National Center for Education Statistics reported a 30.8 percent increase in adult education participants from 1969 to 1975 for an average annual increase of 4.6 percent. The adult population increased 12.6 percent (2.0 percent average annual increase) during the same six-year period.[19]

It is interesting to note that the increase in participation in adult education is greater among older adults than it is for the adult population as a whole. For example, there was a 55.2 percent (7.6 percent average annual rate) increase of participants who were fifty-five years of age and over from 1969–1975. The total population for this age group increased 11.5 percent (1.8 percent annual average).[20]

An update of this study showed an increase of all persons fifty-five and over who were participating in adult education. For example, 2.9 percent participated in 1969. In 1972, 3.5 percent participated; in 1975 the percentage had increased to 4.0 percent. More recent statistics show that in 1978, 4.4 percent of the fifty-five and over population participated in adult education. Of that 4.4 percent, 38.9 percent were male and 61.1 percent were female. Of those sixty-five and over 31 percent were male and 69 percent were female.[21]

It was not until 1950 that the field of adult education became professionalized to the point that the Adult Education Association of the USA was formed. During the decades of the 1950s and 1960s there was considerable foundation support for developing programs to enable adults to engage in continuing education.[22] The Adult Education Act of 1965 expanded educational opportunities for adults in order to raise their basic educational level, improve literacy, and to provide occupational education. In 1976 a new program of lifelong learning for persons who were outside the traditional, sequential educational system was established with the passage of the Higher Education Act Amendment, Title I.[23]

There have been serious barriers[24] which hindered and continue to hinder developments in the field of adult education. There has always been a sense in which adult education has been marginal in the development of the educational system in the United States.

This marginality was no doubt due to a variety of factors. Education, indeed the entire culture, has been youth-oriented. One has only to look at advertising to see that looking and acting young is the norm. Money, then, has been much more readily available for the education of children than for the continuing education of adults. A lack of professionalism and an unstable teaching staff, as well as the need to depend on an enrollment economy, have contributed to its marginal status.

There has often been a lack of coordinated programing in adult education. This is a natural outcome in a field with many and varied providers—most of whom have functions more central to their existence than offering adult education classes. Providers include public schools, community colleges, colleges and universities, cooperative extension services, proprietary schools and consulting firms, libraries, museums, businesses, industry, and religious institutions.

In addition, educational philosophy and methodology have changed dramatically over the years. Many adults may be reticent to return to the classroom either because they did not like it in the past or because they fear they could not succeed in the present. Education as they knew it probably emphasized rote learning of specific knowledge. Today there is much more emphasis on the process—learning to learn so that persons can continue to cope with the knowledge explosion and our fast-changing world.

Some adults find it necessary to become involved in learning opportunities due to job requirements. Currently, a number of occupations and professions (e.g., realtors, funeral directors, nurses, clinical psychologists) are requiring continuing education credit in the form of CEU's[25] for relicensure. Requiring continuing education brings new opportunities as well as a host of problems, and it is yet to be seen whether this will be a benefit or a detriment to the field of adult education.[26]

CEU's are also offered for a wide range of avocational, leisure-time and self-growth topics by various types of providers. Continuing education classes for adults which do not carry any official credit may be sponsored by providers like businesses and industry (e.g., financial planning, wills and annuities, sewing and knitting, etc.), and by nonprofit agencies like Y's, hospitals, schools, churches and synagogues (e.g., exercising, developing self-esteem, natural childbirth, Bible studies, and sign language).

The church is a major provider of adult education opportunities. Malcolm Knowles estimated that in 1955, 15,500,000 adult education participants out of a total of 49,508,000 were involved in education programs sponsored by religious institutions.[27] That this trend continues to the present is reflected in Louis Harris and Associates' comprehensive survey for the National Council on Aging which was published in 1975. That survey reported that older adults were as apt to be participating in courses of fered by churches as in courses offered by colleges or universities.[28]

Dick Murray[29] pointed out in 1981 that 25 to 50 percent of all adult church members are generally enrolled in church-sponsored classes. Sunday School classes are most numerous in the south and southwest but they remain strong in the midwest as well. There are probably more adults in Sunday School classes, Murray maintains, than in any other facet of adult education in the United States.

While a small percentage of all older adults participate in adult education of any type, it is significant to note that church and synagogue are the single most important provider of adult education for older adults. This suggests that a serious examination of the educational needs of older adults might enable religious institutions to build upon their existing foundation in order to more effectively meet those needs.

Who Are the Adults in Adult Education?

Numerous studies have been done to discover what motivates adults to engage in organized learning activities. At present, most of the data that is available results form sociodemographic analysis. We have a reasonably accurate picture of who the adult education participants are as indicated in Table 2.2. It is clear that white persons with more education and higher incomes participate to a greater degree than do blacks and the poor and less well educated. Young and middle-aged adults participate more than do persons fifty-five and over.[30]

As K. Patricia Cross observes, virtually all studies indicate that the more education persons have had, the more apt they are to participate in adult education opportunities.[31] My own study of older rural adults in northwest Iowa suggests caution, however, when applying this generalization to older adults in rural environments. It may be that the value one places on education is a much more important factor affecting participation in adult education than the level of education one has attained. For instance, education was seen by many older rural persons in my study as a process that widens horizons and also makes persons more poised and self-confident. Level of education attained for rural persons born before 1925 may be a result of family

Table 2.2[32]
Participation Rates in Organized Instruction in 1978

	Participation rate[a] (percentages)
Age	
17–34	15.7
35–54	13.0
55 and over	4.5
Sex	
Male	10.7
Female	12.7
Race	
Black	5.8
White	12.5
Educational Attainment	
Less than four years of high school	3.5
Four years of high school	10.7
One to three years of college	18.1
Four or more years of college	27.6
Annual Family Income (dollars)	
Under 5,000	4.9
5,000–7,499	6.3
7,500–9,999	9.7
10,000–14,999	11.3
15,000–24,999	15.1
25,000 and over	18.3
Employment Status	
Employed	15.2
Looking for work	10.3
Keeping house	8.0

[a]NCES made substantial changes in the 1978 survey. The figures cited here are calculated by the "new method," which, unfortunately, is not directly comparable to data from previous triennial surveys.

Source: National Center for Education Statistics, 1980.

size, accessibility of high schools and colleges, economic circumstances, including the depression, and parental attitudes toward education of daughters as compared with sons; it may have little relationship to one's desire and aptitude for education.[33]

Several explanations are offered for the low participation rate in adult education by persons fifty-five and over. There is less need for career-related education and new credentials. Many older persons believe they are too old to learn. Lack of transportation and/or mobility also presents a barrier for some older adults.[34] Barriers will be discussed in chapter three.

Nevertheless, as we have shown, the level of participation among older adults is increasing more rapidly than it is for all adults. There is reason for optimism that participation can be increased even more.

Why Adults Have Participated in Adult Education

Numerous methods have been used in a variety of studies to seek to understand why adults participate in adult education classes. Paul Burgess[35] has pointed out that researchers have approached the task of determining why adults participate in adult education from at least four different perspectives. They have 1) inferred reasons from an analysis of the kinds of educational activities that adults engage in; 2) asked adult learners to tell researchers why they participate; 3) asked adult learners to choose among possible options listed in a questionnaire; and 4) concentrated on the adult's orientation to learning. The results of these studies have the potential for being particularly important for program planners as well as for teachers of adults.

The Learning Orientation Approach

Cyril Houle reported on reasons adults participate in adult education in a pioneering study, *The Inquiring Mind.*[36] He emphasized a learning orientation approach which focused on a major principle or emphasis that gave meaning and direction to a person's learning activity. He identified a three-factor typology which included goal-oriented learners, activity-oriented learners, and learning-oriented learners. Houle's study was based on interviews with twenty-two adult education participants. Goal-oriented learners saw educational participation as "a means of accomplishing fairly clear-cut objectives." Activity-oriented learners participated in education for reasons that had little or no connection with either "the content or the announced purposes of the activity." Finally, Houle described learning-oriented learners as those who "seek knowledge for its own sake." He made it clear that these three orientations are not clearly distinguishable from each other. Rather, they represent a central emphasis regarding individuals' reasons for participating in adult education.

Researchers have built upon Cyril Houle's study by examining motivational orientations of adult learners.[37] These studies used a factor-analytic approach to identify adults' orientations to learning.[38] Basically, these studies yielded lists of factors which were seen as refining, while being consistent with, Houle's typology (see Table 2.3).

Roger Boshier's study which was done in New Zealand indicated that, in reality, all adult education participants may be "goal-oriented" in that they are motivated either by

Table 2.3[39]
Summary of Factors Identified in Studies of Learning Orientations and Their
Relationship to Houle's Typology

| | Houle's Orientations | | |
Study	Goal orientation	Activity orientation	Learning orientation
Sheffield	Personal goal Societal goal	Need fulfillment Sociability	Learning

Boshier	Other-directed
	  advancement
		Social contact
		Self- vs. other-
		  centeredness
			Educational
			  preparation

Morstain and
Smart
	External
	  expectations
	Professional
	  advancement
	Social welfare
		Social relationships
		Escape/stimulation
			Cognitive
			  interest

Burgess	Personal goal Social goal Religious goal Meet formal requirements	Social activity Escape	Desire to know

deficiency needs or growth needs. He reported "a shift away from pragmatic and utilitarian reasons as people get older."[40]

Paul Burgess' study, based on 1,046 usable responses from adult education participants in fifty-four different classes in the St. Louis area yielded seven factors which accounted for 63.1 percent of the variance. Those seven factors were: 1) the desire to know; 2) the desire to reach a personal goal; 3) the desire to reach a social goal; 4) the desire to reach a religious goal; 5) the desire to take part in social activity; 6) the desire to escape; and 7) the desire to meet formal requirements.[41]

This is the only study of those cited which identified religion as a factor. Burgess suggested that one possible explanation is that items reflecting this orientation were not included in the instruments which other studies used.

It is apparent that the religious components which have emerged are much less well-developed and systematized than most other factors. In addition, they seem to be closely tied to concern for institutionalized religion. For example, Burgess' three miscellaneous items which emerged as factor four included such diverse statements as "the desire to reach a religious goal," being "better able to serve a church," and having an "interest in mission work." The third item referred to improving one's "spiritual well-being."[42]

Barry Morstain and John Smart[43] replicated and expanded Roger Boshier's study by seeking to discover what significant differences might result based on sex-age groupings. This study of 611 adult education students from one college organized the data around the following six factors: 1) social relationships; 2) external expectations; 3) social welfare; 4) professional advancement; 5) escape-stimulation; and 6) cognitive interest. Male-female score differences increased with age and became most striking with the forty-two and over group.

The clear emergence of mixed reasons for persons' participation in adult education in this study by Morstain and Smart gives additional credence to another similar conclusion by Boshier that the motivational factors or reasons persons give to explain their participation in adult education are somewhat more complex than Houle's three orientations may suggest.

Roger Boshier gradually moved away from the Houle tradition toward a model that focused more on the "social and psychological underpinnings of reasons for participation."[44] He began examining self-concept as an important factor in understanding self-actualizing behavior. While continuing to use a factor-analytical methodology with the *Education Participation Scale,* he sought to find relationships to social and psychological variables which seemed to be important factors that affected participation. His study began a move toward a more holistic approach to the study of reasons by taking cognizance of social factors, in addition to an individual's motives or reasons.

An Empirical Study

In an exploratory study,[45] I examined and compared the accounts older adults gave to significant others to legitimize their participation in adult education sponsored by churches and/or by schools. Data were gathered through focused interviews in order to understand their reasons. Reasons were examined in light of the older adults' self-image, their past experiences with education and religion, and their social context.

To be Educated Is . . .

The older adults in my study tended to view being educated as something quite separate from the amount of formal education or the number of degrees that persons have achieved. Being educated was understood as a process that is reflected in all of one's life.

Education was believed to enable persons to develop poise and to become more self-assured. It was seen as relative; this viewpoint was expressed by one participant who observed that there is no point at which you can say a person is or isn't educated.

Education is something persons can experience in a wide variety of settings and ways. It should generally lead to widened horizons and a more inclusive approach to life.

Adult Education Should . . .

There was a wide range of responses among the participants in this study when they were asked how important adult education was to them and what they expected to gain from it. Some expected nothing more than to fill some time; others believed that it was vitally important and that they couldn't get along without it.

Those who valued adult education classes as significant believed that it broadened their minds. Several expected to gain new knowledge. One highly educated man observed that his church-school class had taught him not to make assumptions based on sophistication or plainness.

We will look at this study in more detail in later chapters when we examine ways to plan with and teach older adults.

Adult Education for the Old

Few studies dealing with reasons persons partipate in adult education have focused on older adults. Many studies did not use age as a variable. However, one study using age as a variable was done; it showed that North Carolina's community colleges and technical institutes were doing an inadequate job of reaching the over-sixty population of that state. The over-sixty learners who David Daniel, et al., studied were found to be "generally social-culturally and improvement-learning oriented toward education." He suggested that the failure to reach this segment of the population may have resulted from not understanding "the value orientations toward education of the 60+ age category."[46]

The Louis Harris national survey isolated reasons which older adults gave for taking courses. These are listed in Table 2.4.

Table 2.4[47]
Reasons Given by Older Adults for Participating in Adult Education

Reasons	Public 55–64 (5%)*	Public 65+ (2%)
To expand your general knowledge about some field or hobby	80%	76%
To acquire job skills	24%	6%
To make good use of your time	49%	39%
To be with other people	44%	28%
Other reasons	—	2%

*Numbers in parentheses refer to the percentage of the total population in this age cohort who participate in adult education. Percentages in the body of the table do not equal 100% because persons could give as many reasons as they wished.

John Johnstone and Ramon Rivera studied adult learners' stated goals at the time of their most recent enrollment in an adult education course. They found a downward trend in vocation-related goals among males aged fifty and over and an apparent desire to focus on things more relevant to retirement. Older people often had as goals "general information, social contacts, and spare-time enjoyment."[48]

It seems reasonable to conclude that the need for goal-oriented learning for older adults will increase, rather than decrease. As older adults face an increasingly complex and technological world, they can now expect to live, on the average, seventeen years beyond retirement.[49] They may well need to develop new skills and to learn additional information.

Those increased leisure years may be filled for some with activity-oriented learning. Some will no doubt turn to adult education as a means to seek to make new friends or to fill empty hours.

Finally, we believe some will turn to religious education as they seek to come to terms with who they are and what life means. It may be that what Houle labeled "learning-oriented learning" is, in fact, the process of seeking to make sense of one's life and of all of life.

The Need for Adult Education in the Future

There are several major forces which have given impetus to this increased interest in adult education. Learning is being viewed as lifelong by necessity. Books like Alvin Toffler's *Future Shock* and *The Third Wave*[50] and John Naisbitt's *Megatrends*[51] illustrate that we are living in a world that embodies rapid and constant change. Adults in our society were not taught how to remain productive in such a world. Ivan Illich[52] and other advocates of liberation have clearly demonstrated that our formal educational institutions have serious deficiencies. Illich and others claim that the poor, the disadvantaged, and those in ethnic minority groups may not have been given the necessary skills to cope with the societal problems they encounter daily in our changing world.[53] It might be added that as the disadvantaged develop more adequate coping skills, the advantaged will need to develop new ways of thinking and acting that are not based on a have/have not mentality.

Occupational obsolescence is a term that is being widely used. Persons entering the job market in the 1980s can expect to change careers from six to eight times during their lifetime.[54]

Rapid changes in technology throughout the world necessitate that education be lifelong. In a deeper sense, persons who are confronted with rapid and constant change must develop and maintain the skills that enable continuing growth and learning if they are to live with meaning in this world. It becomes less and less satisfactory to rely on finding one's answers to the questions "Who am I?" and "Where is my worth?" through one's occupation. "I am a farmer" or "I am a professor's wife" are much less secure and lasting seats for one's security than was once believed to be true.

The breakdown of the nuclear family, divorce, changing economic circumstances of business and industry, increasingly complex technologies and political upheavals are all very apparent. This fact makes it clear that *finding* answers and *making* adjustments are more important than any given answer or adjustment. Learning to learn, acquiring needed information, and developing new skills are vital. Being able to make wise decisions and then being willing to change them when situations require it are abilities persons need in order to grow toward wholeness. The *process* called living, which is described here, demands that adults at all stages of life continue to be learners. What form that education for living should or will take is an open question. But the fact that adult education throughout the life span is a necessity cannot be denied.

If adult education in the future is to meet the needs of

older adults, there are several prerequisites which must be met. Burton Clark[55] observed that institutional integrity must be established and maintained if adult education is to thrive. That requires being clear about organizational self-definition and being able to maintain autonomy from outside pressures. Even more important, there must be congruence between a sound philosophy of adult education and the organizational and methodological practice of adult education.

Chapter Two Notes

1. Samuel Eliot Morison, *The Founding of Harvard College* (Cambridge: Harvard University Press, 1935), p. 45.

2. Malcolm S. Knowles, *The Adult Education Movement in the United States,* rev. ed. (Huntington,New York: Robert E. Kreiger Publishing Co., 1977), p. 3.

3. Ibid., p. 4.

4. Ibid., pp. 4–24.

5. Ibid., pp. 8–9.

6. Robert W. Lynn and Elliot Wright, *The Big Little School: 200 Years of the Sunday School,* rev. ed. (Birmingham, Alabama: Religious Education Press, 1980), p. 44.

7. Paul H. Vieth, *The Church and Christian Education* (St. Louis: The Bethany Press, 1947), pp. 264–270. Also see C. B. Eavey, *The History of Christian Education* (Chicago: Moody Press, 1964).

8. Lynn and Wright, *The Big Little School,* p. 20.

9. Frederick Rudolph, *The American College and University: A History* (New York: Vintage Books, 1962), pp. 241–263.

10. This section is based on material included in Joseph E. Gould, *The Chautauqua Movement* (Albany: State University of New York Press, 1961) and Theodore Morrison, *Chautauqua: A Center for Education, Religion, and the Arts in America* (Chicago: The University of Chicago Press, 1974).

11. James D. Smart, *The Teaching Ministry of the Church* (Philadelphia: Westminster Press, 1954), p. 54.

12. Knowles, *The Adult Education Movement in the United States,* pp. 36–38.

13. John Skow, "In New York State: Culture's Front Porch," *Time*, Vol. 120, No. 5 (August 2, 1982), pp. 8–9.

14. Knowles, *The Adult Education Movement in the United States*, p. 55.

15. From Diana K. Harris and William E. Cole, *Sociology of Aging*, p. 303. Copyright (c) 1980 by Houghton Mifflin Company. Used by permission.

16. Ibid. Also see Knowles, *The Adult Education Movement in the United States*, chapter 8.

17. Knowles, *A History of the Adult Education Movement in the United States*, pp. 269–279.

18. R. Cortwright and W. Brice, "Adult Basic Education," in R. M. Smith, G. F. Aker, and J. R. Kidd, eds., *Handbook of Adult Education* (New York: Macmillan, 1970), p. 407.

19. National Center for Education Statistics, *Participation in Adult Education Final Report 1975* Washington, D.C.: U.S. Department of Health, Education, and Welfare, 1978), p. 4.

20. Ibid.

21. "Statistical Notes" (Washington, D.C.: Clearinghouse on Aging, Administration on Aging, No. 6, January, 1981).

22. For example, the Carnegie Corporation, the Kellogg Foundation, and the Mott Foundation were supportive of these endeavors.

23. John R. Verduin, Jr., Harry G. Miller, and Charles E. Greer, *Adults Teaching Adults* (Austin, Texas: Learning Concepts, 1977), pp. 43–45.

24. See Roger Hiemstra, *Lifelong Learning* (Lincoln, Nebraska: Professional Educators Publications, Inc., 1976), chapter 2; Burton R. Clark, *Adult Education in Transition: A Study of Institutional Insecurity* (University of California Publications in Sociology and Social Institutions, Vol. I, No. 2., Berkeley: University of California Press, 1956).

25. Continuing Education Units are widely used by a number of professions. One CEU (1.0) equals ten hours of instruction (or in some cases, ten fifty-minute periods).

26. For example, see K. Patricia Cross, *Adults As Learners* (San Francisco: Jossey-Bass Publishers, 1981), pp. 40–46, where she discusses "mandated" continuing education. Key questions revolve around the right to coerce free American citizens into education, the effectiveness of compulsory education, and who should be responsible for developing and enforcing professional standards.

27. Knowles, *A History of the Adult Education Movement in the United States*, p. 251.

28. Louis Harris and Associates, *The Myths and Reality of Aging in America* (Washington, D.C.: The National Council on the Aging, Inc., 1975), p. 109. This is confirmed by Roger Hiemstra in *Lifelong Learning* when he

says that, in 1972, 32.9 percent of the total adult education participant population participated in church sponsored adult education while half of those over 55 were engaged in church sponsored classes.

29. Dick Murray, *Strengthening the Adult Sunday School Class* (Nashville, Tennessee: Abingdon, 1981).

30. For a detailed discussion of who participates in adult learning see Cross, *Adults as Learners,* pp. 50–80.

31. Ibid., p. 54. Permission to quote granted by Jossey-Bass Publishers.

32. Ibid., pp. 54–55.

33. Linda Jane Vogel, "How Older Adults Perceive and Legitimize their Adult Education Participation in Schools and Churches" (Unpublished doctoral dissertation, The University of Iowa, 1981), pp. 106–108.

34. Cross, *Adults as Learners,* pp. 57–58.

35. Paul D. Burgess, "Reasons for Adult Participation in Group Educational Activities," *Adult Education,* Vol. XXII, No. 1 (1971), pp. 3–29.

36. Cyril O. Houle, *The Inquiring Mind* (Madison, Wisconsin: The University of Wisconsin Press, 1961).

37. Sherman B. Sheffield, "The Orientations of Adult Continuing Learners," in Daniel Solomon, ed., *The Continuing Learner* (Chicago: The Center for the Study of Liberal Education for Adults, 1964); Paul D. Burgess, "Reasons for Adult Education Participation in Group Educational Activities," *Adult Education,* Vol. XXII, No. 1, (1971); Roger Boshier, "Motivational Orientations of Adult Education Participants: A Factor Analytic Exploration of Houle's Typology," *Adult Education,* Vol. XXI, No. 2 (1971); Barry R. Morstain and John C. Smart, "Reasons for Participation in Adult Education Courses: A Multivariate Analysis of Group Differences," *Adult Education,* Vol. 24, No. 2 (1974): Gary Dickinson and Kathleen M. Clark, "Learning Orientations and Participation in Self-Education and Continuing Education," *Adult Education,* Vol. XXVI, No. 1 (1975).

38. A critical analysis of this methodology as it has been applied in fourteen different motivational studies can be found in an article by Roger Boshier, "Factor Analysts at Large: A Critical Review of the Motivational Orientation Literature," *Adult Education,* Vol. XXVII, No. 1 (1976), pp. 24–47.

39. Dickinson and Clark, "Learning Orientations and Participation in Self-Education and Continuing Education," p. 7. Permission to quote granted by the American Association for Adult and Continuing Education (AAACE).

40. Roger Boshier, "Motivational Orientations of Adult Education

Participants: A Factor Analytic Exploration of Houle's Typology," *Adult Education*, Vol. XXI, No. 2 (1971) pp. 3–26.

41. Burgess, "Reasons for Adult Education Participation in Group Educational Activities," p. 18.

42. Ibid., p. 23.

43. Morstain and Smart, "Reasons for Participation in Adult Education Courses," pp. 83–93.

44. Roger Boshier, "Motivational Orientations Re-Visited: Life-Space Motives and the Education Participation Scale," *Adult Education*, Vol. XXVII, No. 2 (1977), pp. 89–115.

45. Vogel, "How Older Adults Perceive and Legitimize their Participation in Adult Education." See Appendix A for information about the participants in this study and the types of classes in which they were participating.

46. David Daniel, Robert Templin, and Ronald Shearon, "The Value Orientations of Older Adults toward Education," *Educational Gerontology*, Vol. 2 (1977), pp. 33–42.

47. Louis Harris and Associates, *The Myths and Realities of Aging in America*, 1975, published by The National Council on the Aging, Inc., p. 108. Quoted with permission.

48. John W. C. Johnstone and Ramon Rivera, *Volunteers for Learning* (Chicago: Aldine, 1965), pp. 143–162.

49. "Myths and Realities" (filmstrip), *Perspectives on Aging* (Costa Mesa, California: Concept Media, 1973).

50. Alvin Toffler, *Future Shock* (New York: Random House, 1970) and *The Third Wave* (New York: William Morrow and Co., 1980).

51. John Naisbitt, *Megatrends: Ten New Directions Transforming Our Lives* (New York: Warner Books, 1982).

52. Ivan Illich, *Deschooling Society* (New York: Harper & Row, 1970).

53. Hiemstra, *Lifelong Learning*, p. 7. Also see Allen J. Moore, "Liberation and the Future of Christian Education," in Jack L. Seymour and Donald E. Miller, *Contemporary Approaches to Christian Education* (Nashville, Tennessee: Abingdon, 1982), pp. 103–122.

54. Malcolm Knowles, "Agenda for the Eighties," *Lifelong Learning*, Vol. III, No. 5 (January, 1980), p. 18.

55. Burton R. Clark, *Adult Education in Transition: A Study of Institutional Insecurity* (Berkeley: University of California Press, 1956).

CHAPTER THREE

How Older Adults Learn

"Old dogs can learn new tricks, but they may be reluctant to do so, particularly when they are not convinced that the new trick is any better than the old tricks which served them so well in the past. They may not learn new tricks as rapidly as they did in the past. But if they started out as clever young pups, they are very likely to end up as wise old hounds" (Ledford Bischof in *Adult Psychology*, p. 224).

Those who study learning must be concerned with defining it and measuring it. They must seek to understand how to foster and enable learning as well as how to identify and remove barriers which block learning.

Learning is reflected in what persons do and who they are. It involves cognitive growth, affective growth, and creativity.

What Is Intelligence?

Intelligence is a topic that has been discussed and debated at great length. What is it? How can it be measured? Does it decrease as persons age?

Often in our society, intelligence is equated with one's

BETHEL SEMINARY WEST
LIBRARY
4747 College Avenue
San Diego, California 92115

score on a standardized IQ test. When one examines the literature on cultural bias and age bias, however, the wisdom of relying greatly on such tests may be questioned.

There are two basic approaches to studying intelligence: the psychometric approach which uses tests to measure intelligence, and the cognitive approach which studies thought processes.[1] Intelligence is highly complex. Some believe that there is, in fact, a biologically-based reality—known in the literature as "g." Others claim that there are several intellectual abilities that are independent of one another. Thurstone developed the Primary Mental Abilities model which tests five independent mental abilities: number, word fluency, verbal meaning, reasoning, and space.[2] Guilford has developed a more complex model that identifies 120 factors.[3] It seems safe to say that intelligence is complex and not easily measured.

While early IQ tests purported to measure general intelligence ("g"), it is now believed that they must, at the very least, include an examination of crystallized intelligence (knowledge gained through experience) and fluid intelligence (native mental ability not dependent on experience or learning).[4]

There are some serious problems regarding psychometric research with older adults which have contributed to the development of a number of misconceptions. Declines in intelligence have been attributed to aging when, in fact, chronological age is not a significant factor in accounting for variance in intellectual aging prior to age sixty or the early seventies.[5]

Traditional IQ tests were generally designed for school-age children or for army inductees to predict abilities for success. There is serious doubt that these tests which were age and purpose specific are appropriate when given to older adults. In addition, inadequate norms exist for older adults, testing procedures ignore the needs and anxieties of older adults, and there is no compensation for the fact that older subjects generally have lower motivation toward testing than do younger subjects.[6]

Most of the data used to make generalizations about intelligence and aging comes from cross-sectional data. This tends to attribute to age what more appropriately ought to be attributed to cohort effect, educational level, or socioeconomic status. In addition, data that uses intelligence data in the form of averages without ranges tends to be misleading.

Some recent longitudinal studies now suggest that intelligence may increase beyond seventy years of age.[7] In general, longitudinal research is preferred over cross-sectional research; certainly this is true when examining what changes occur with aging.

Nevertheless, it is important not to err in the opposite direction by putting too much stock in these initial longitudinal studies on intelligence among the old. One of the pitfalls in longitudinal research on intelligence, especially involving aged subjects, is the effect of selective attrition.[8] Those persons who are less healthy or less motivated tend to drop out of the study. They seem to be the most likely candidates to test at lower intelligence levels, and, since they tend to drop out, the finding may appear higher than is actually the case.

It seems clear from both cross-sectional and longitudinal research data that intelligence is a "very plastic variable." It is multidimensional, modifiable, and interactive with other persons and one's environment.[9] There can be no doubt that, barring serious illness, older adults can learn and grow.

Perhaps a more fruitful way of studying intelligence would be to approach it contextually and to examine how persons adapt to the tasks they face each day. This approach may be most fruitful in terms of understanding intelligence and the old. It requires reflecting on the active interplay between a person's actions and the context or environment where the actions take place.[10]

Sherry Willis and Paul Baltes have developed a multicausal and interactive model which may be helpful at this point.[11] They suggest that the interaction of biological factors and environmental factors are the basic determinants of human development. In addition, there are three important influences on development which interact.

Age-graded influences are described as fairly normative and predictable in that they are related to biological maturation and age-graded social norms. Examples of age-graded influences include marriage, child-rearing years, retirement, and persons' advances in occupation.

History-graded influences relate to cohort differences. Examples of history-graded influences affecting persons who are elderly today would include the depression of the 1930s and World War II.

Nonnormative influences are extremely personalized and are, therefore, not predictable. Examples can be found from individual life histories and include such events as important honors and awards, accidents and illnesses, losses through divorce or death, and significant relationships.

These three areas of influence interact with basic determinants as indicated in figure 3.1. This multicausal and interactive model can aid us in developing a contextual understanding of intelligence that is more comprehensive than a cognitive approach and that is both more compre-

Figure 3.1[12]
Influences on Life-span Development

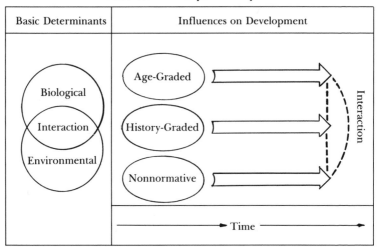

Basic Determinants	Influences on Development

Three sources of influence on life-span development that cumulate and interact over time (adapted from Baltes, 1979; Baltes, Cornelius, & Nesselroade, 1979).

hensive and less dependent on test data than a psychometric approach.

What Is Affective Learning?

Affective learning has to do with the emotional aspects of one's life. It includes our tastes, preferences, values, attitudes, and morals. When one holds a holistic view of persons, the emotional is as important as the cognitive in understanding education.

Learning in a holistic sense must be relational. It has to do with acknowledging and owning one's own values and feelings as one becomes more fully who one is and can be.[13]

Persons who acknowledge the importance of the affective in teaching and learning generally emphasize personal growth. This necessitates encouraging exploration rather than mere acceptance. It encourages active learning which values freedom over conformity, growth over maintenance, and change over the status quo. It goes beyond facts to emphasize meanings.[14]

Self-actualization can never be simply cognitive. It involves both the cognitive and the affective; it necessitates creative expression that manifests itself through the personality in whatever activities persons undertake.[15]

Education that is holistic must concern itself with enabling wholeness. That means that it must deal with persons' basic self-concepts. How persons perceive themselves does affect what and how persons learn.

Certainly, religious education must include the affective. Lewis Sherrill asserts that one of the goals of Christian religious education is to enable persons to "attain increasing self-understanding and self-knowledge and an increasing realization of their own potentialities." This can lead toward building relationships and accepting responsibilities as God's children.[16]

It is important to reiterate that attitudes, values, and morals have both cognitive and affective components. Likewise, cognitive content carries affective content and elicits affective as well as cognitive responses. Education that seeks to enable growth toward wholeness and self-actualization must deal consciously with affective learning.

What Is Creativity?

According to J. P. Guilford, psychologists generally agree that all persons possess some potential for creativity.[17]

Creativity seems to involve factors like 1) exhibiting a certain sensitivity to problems, 2) having both nonverbal and verbal fluency, 3) having novel ideas, 4) exhibiting flexibility of mind, 5) demonstrating synthesizing and analyzing ability, 6) being able to reorganize and redefine the whole, 7) dealing with complexity, and 8) being able to engage in evaluation.[18] For Guilford, creativity is associated with the ability to engage in divergent thinking.

Guilford maintains that creativity can be developed through education. He points out that even if we were to raise the creativity level of average people by a small percentage, there could be great social consequences.[19]

Another approach to creativity has been to study individuals in a variety of fields to determine the age where creativity seems to peak. In general, persons tend to exhibit the greatest creativity in their thirties; by the time persons reach fifty, 80 percent have completed their most creative work. In the humanities, however, seventy year-olds have been judged to be as creative as forty year-olds.[20]

There can be no doubt that older adults are capable of making creative contributions to society. Michelangelo painted *The Last Judgment* when he was sixty-six; he was seventy when he finished painting the dome in St. Peter's Cathedral in Rome. At eighty-two, Goethe completed *Faust*. Wilhelm Wundt, remembered as the father of psychology as we know it today, completed his ten volume work on social psychology when he was eighty-eight. Winston Churchill headed the British government in his seventies and George Meany headed the AFL-CIO into his eighties.[21]

These well-known persons cannot be dismissed as extraordinary exceptions. Most of us could name several older persons from our own local communities who continue to make creative contributions. Anyone who has had anything to do with Elderhostel, a nationwide program providing residential learning experiences for over 55,000 persons aged sixty and over in more than 600 colleges and universities each year, knows that creativity, as well as a desire and ability to learn, is very much present in the lives of older adults.

Learning in Adulthood vs. Learning in Childhood

Every issue is many-faceted. The issue revolving around the differences and similarities between the ways adults learn and the ways children learn is no exception. J. R. Kidd rightly observes that, on the one hand, the differences that distinguish adult learners from children are great; at the same time, there are many continuities in learning throughout the life span.[22]

Malcolm Knowles is well-known for his writings on the topic of pedagogy (education of children) vs. andragogy (education of adults). It is unfortunate that such a strong dichotomy was drawn, and in recent years Knowles has moved toward seeing education as a continuum that moves from pedagogy toward andragogy.[23]

Andragogy is defined by Knowles as "the art and science of helping adults learn." It refers to a teaching and learning process that is based on four basic assumptions which he claims apply to adults but do not apply to children. They are: 1) maturing adults move from "being a dependent personality" toward being "a self-directing human being"; 2) their increasing experience provides a growing "resource for learning"; 3) learning readiness is in response to the developmental tasks of adults' social roles; and 4) adult learners want immediate application from learning rather than possessing a willingness to postpone application of what is learned.[24]

Table 3.2[25]

Comparison of Assumptions and Designs of Pedagogy and Andragogy

Assumptions

	Pedagogy	Andragogy
Self-concept	Dependency	Increasing self-directiveness
Experience	Of little worth	Learners are a rich resource for learning
Readiness	Biological Development, social pressure	Developmental tasks of social roles
Time perspective	Postponed application	Immediacy of application
Orientation to learning	Subject-centered	Problem-centered

Design elements

	Pedagogy	Andragogy
Climate	Authority-oriented, formal, competitive	Mutuality, respectful, collaborative, informal
Planning	By teacher	Mechanism for mutual planning
Diagnosis of needs	By teacher	Mutual self-diagnosis
Formulation of objectives	By teacher	Mutual negotiation
Design	Logic of the subject matter; content units	Sequenced in terms of readiness; problem units
Activities	Transmittal techniques	Experiential techniques (inquiry)
Evaluation	By teacher	Mutual rediagnosis of needs; mutual measurement of program

Table 3.2 delineates the assumptions of pedagogy and andragogy as they were developed by Knowles in 1978. Examining the differences is helpful in understanding the historical development of the concept of andragogy. It is my belief that the principles of andragogy, understood in the context of the differing developmental needs and skills of persons—children, youth, young adults, middle-aged adults, and older adults—may provide a firm foundation for developing educational plans for all ages.

Serious questions have been raised regarding the sharp dichotomies which Malcolm Knowles makes between the orientations to learning (subject-centered vs. problem-centered), and the role experience plays in the learning process. His assumptions about pedagogy seem to me to be indefensible. It is my belief that the assumptions Knowles makes about andragogy are appropriate for learners of all ages so long as we take into account learners' developmental levels. For example, it is possible and desirable to assume *"increasing* self-directiveness" for three-year-olds as well as for adults. Teachable moments enhance learning for children as well as adults. "Mutuality, respectful and collaborative" climates that meet learners where they are seem to be better than "authority-oriented" climates regardless of age.

For our purposes, we will focus on the concept of andragogy as we seek to develop a process for enabling the religious education of older adults.[26]

How Do Older Adults Learn?

Questions are being raised regarding the possible reasons why earlier studies have shown that after age sixty-five, older persons generally do not learn as well as younger persons. Researchers are suggesting that timed tests definitely put the aged at a disadvantage since their pace of learning is demonstrably slower. Motivation seems to be a problem and older adults appear to be less willing to engage in seemingly meaningless tasks. K. Warner Schaie and James Geiwitz contend that when older adults are given enough time, the atmosphere is relaxed, and the task is meaningful and relatively simple, there is almost no diference in learning ability between the very old and the very young.[27]

This section might have been paraphrased, "How Do Older Adults Forget?" if we were basing it on today's common lore about aging. When persons forget something, one expects to hear them say, "I must be getting old!"

When we examine how persons learn and remember, the learning process is different from what we may have supposed. We will also see where in the learning process some older persons seem to experience difficulty.

K. Warner Schaie and James Geiwitz have diagramed the memory system as illustrated in figure 3.3.

Stimuli come to us from external sources and we receive it through our senses by hearing it, seeing it, smelling it, or feeling it. Psychologists have used the term "encoding" to describe this receiving or learning process.

Once received, the data must be stored; psychologists often speak of "sensory storage" as the place where the sensory images can be stored for a very brief time. Diagram 3.3 indicates that the memory has a relatively small capacity for short-term storage. Data stored here has not been processed or organized to any great degree. However, persons are able to recall this data and they may process it by transferring it to long-term storage.

Humans have an extremely large capacity for long-term

Figure 3.3[28]
Human Memory

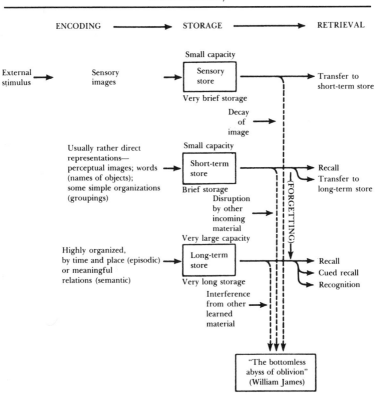

The memory system—a very rough approximation of current memory theories. The primary purpose of this chart is to illustrate two basic dimensions: 1) the three phases of memory (encoding, storage, retrieval), and 2) the three storage systems (sensory, short-term, long-term). The additional material is included to give some idea of the hypothetical differences in encoding, storage, retrieval, and forgetting for the three stores.

storage and can store data there rather permanently. The data is highly organized, using either episodic (time and place) or semantic (meaningful relationship apart from any context) rubrics. From long-term storage persons are able to recall data ("Pete was born in 1965"), to retrieve it through cued recall ("Of course, Mark is twelve years younger than I am so he was born in 1952."), or to recognize that we know something when we hear it or see it again ("Of course, I know Mahler's Fifth Symphony—I just didn't remember I did until I heard it again!"). Retrieval of material can be hampered by interference from other learned material and may, for all practical purposes, have been lost in "the bottomless abyss of oblivion."

Here again, existing research which deals with learning and aging is mostly cross-sectional and often focuses on memory. Until we find ways to study encoding as well as retrieval, it cannot be made clear whether there is a decline in learning and/or in memory.

It seems clear that retrieval can be effectively improved if the data received for encoding can be organized. Some studies have shown that, when aided in organizing the data, older subjects improve in comparison to younger subjects. In addition, when shown how to process data at shallow, medium, and deep levels, older adults learned as well as or better than younger adults.[29]

Some are now maintaining that older adults require more time to encode data. They also seem to have more difficulty in forming associations and spontaneously organizing data.[30]

In fact, it is quite possible that there is an important history-graded influence at work here. It may be that the emphasis on rote learning, which characterized schooling when today's older adults were students, puts them at a distinct disadvantage when they are compared with younger persons whose education focused more on the thinking process and on organizing and classifying information.

Turning our attention to the retrieval process, it is generally agreed that memory is most clear immediately following an experience. It tends to decline systematically as time passes. The ability to recall an experience is lost more quickly than the ability to recognize it. In spite of existing myths to the contrary, this holds true for old adults as well as young adults.[31]

How, then, do we explain the belief that many old persons can remember the past in great detail while they can remember very little of the present? K. Warner Schaie and James Geiwitz offer several reasonable explanations. Old memories may be strengthened by engaging in the processes of reenacting and reminiscing. Difficulties in encoding in the present may result from outside interferences, a lack of motivation to remember, and sensory or ability losses. In some cases, changes in brain functioning may be responsible but this deficiency should not be perceived as a result of aging, per se. For example, dementia may hinder or block one's ability to remember, but that is a condition that results from biological changes which are not directly related to the aging process.[32]

Whatever the problems individual persons may encounter, adults at every age can learn and can profit from educational opportunities. In a fast-changing world where, on the average, persons can expect to live seventeen years after they have retired, planned educational experiences can provide growth producing and life-enhancing opportunities.

Robert Havighurst maintains that when persons over seventy-five participate in adult learning activities they are likely to have a personal need which they are seeking to meet. Those needs may be 1) to experience life with "dignity, self-control and comfort," 2) to find a satisfying and enjoyable activity, 3) to continue to be a contributing member of society, 4) to maintain interaction with younger people, or 5) to remain vitally alive physically and mentally.[33]

A word needs to be said about the frail-old—those persons who are less able to be independent and who may reside in nursing homes. They, too, are capable of learning and can benefit from educational opportunities. Irene Burnside[34] maintains that these persons need more direction and support; they prefer a nonconfrontive, learning situation.

Growing Toward Self-Actualization

As persons seek to grow toward self-actualization, they must contend with their abilities and their motivation. Motivation can be intrinsic—arising from within the learner (e.g., pursuing personal interests and exploring one's environment); motivation can also be extrinsic—arising from sources outside the learner (e.g., responding to approval and/or disapproval).[35]

Education that is person-centered and focuses more on the learning process than on the content or the outcomes, seeks to emphasize intrinsic motivation. A basic presupposition underlying this approach is that all persons have the potential for becoming "complete, authentic, autonomous, 'congruent' or 'fully functioning' persons."[36]

Building on Sherry Willis and Paul Baltes' multicausal and interactive model for understanding human development (refer to Figure 3.2), we might gain insights by examining Roger Boshier's congruence model.[37] He maintains that persons' motivation for learning grows out of their perception and interpretation of their internal psychological factors and the external environmental factors in their worlds.

The desire to participate or the propensity not to participate or to drop out is dependent upon the congruence/discrepancy between the person's self-concept and the factors that make up the educational environment. For example, a person who feels good about self and is comfortable in, and feels affirmed by, a particular educational environment (e.g., location, leader, subject-matter, other participants) will be likely to begin and to continue in that experience. Congruence is maintained.

When many incongruencies exist, persons probably will not begin to participate. Dropouts are most likely to be those who experience a greater sense of discrepancies than of congruence. This holds true for all kinds of groups and situations where older adults engage in planned learning.

One clear implication of this theory is that greater attention must be paid to achieving a proper match between potential adult learners and the learning environment. Another important point relates to what was said in chapter one about the importance of one's self-concept or self-esteem. Persons with poor self-concepts or low self-esteem are less likely to experience congruence with any external environment and must be aided in developing self-esteem if they are to become viable candidates for adult education participation.

Additional insights can be gained by reading the works of phenomenologically oriented psychologists like Abraham Maslow and Carl Rogers who foster a humanistic approach to adult education.[38] Their writings suggest that persons can grow toward self-actualization—a state where there is increasing congruence between persons' real selves and their ideal selves. Carl Rogers describes self-actualization as the urge in all persons "to expand, extend, become autonomous, develop, and mature."[39]

Abraham Maslow (see Figure 3.4), through his well-known hierarchy of needs, maintains that physiological needs (e.g., hunger, sex) are most basic and that these must be satisfied before one can be concerned with forms of behavior that are higher on the heirarchy. Safety needs (e.g., shelter, consistency) can be addressed when one's physiological needs are met.

The third level of the hierarchical triangle involves needs for love and belonging. Then esteem needs (e.g., self-respect, respect from others) may be met. Only those persons whose survival needs are clearly met, who are comfortable

Figure 3.4
Maslow's Hierarchy of Needs

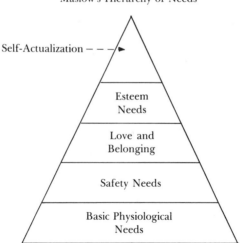

in their vocation and have mutually satisfying social interaction, and who have developed good self-esteem are able to become self-actualized persons. Self-actualization is growth motivated rather than deficiency motivated and can be understood as "the desire to become more and more what one is, to become everything that one is capable of becoming."[40]

Lewis Sherrill builds on these insights when he maintains that at any given time every person is an existing self and also a potential self—that is, the self one can become. All persons are potentially capable of entering into loving relationships, of liberation, of participating in community, of being a unique individual, of wholeness, of creativity, and of growth. Everyone is "both a being and a becoming."[41]

Barriers to Learning

Basic barriers to adult learning may be seen in philosophical and theological terms, as well as in psychological terms. Paul Tillich speaks of the "anxiety of fate and death," "the anxiety of emptiness and meaninglessness" and "the anxiety of guilt and condemnation."[42] Historian Arnold Toynbee uses the term "schisms in the soul" to describe the fragmentation of persons which prevents wholeness.[43] There are basic threats to the self which may block our becoming what we can be, if they are not faced and understood.[44]

Barriers to adult learning[45], like reasons for participation, are not easy to study. One might legitimately ask whether persons are even conscious of their reasons for nonparticipation. It is generally agreed, however, that barriers that hinder or block adult learning can be grouped into three general categories.

Situational barriers grow out of nonnormative influences

in an individual's life. For older persons, these may include inadequate financial resources or a lack of transportation.

Institutional barriers may spring from the environmental determinants in the multicausal and interactive model of adult development. Scheduling learning experiences at night or in locations that must be reached by climbing several flights of stairs may be institutional barriers for older adults. Prerequisite requirements which ignore life experiences, strict attendance requirements, or involved and unclear enrollment procedures may also block participation.

Finally, dispositional barriers which grow directly out of one's self-concept may hinder or block educational participation. For example, feelings of personal inadequacy or a fear of failing may block participation. Fear that one is too old to learn or having done poorly in school in the past may be barriers that are seen by the person as too great to overcome.

That barriers do exist cannot be denied. However, the most productive approach for us to take will be to focus on assessed needs of older adults. Then we can build a model for adult learning that seeks to develop and maintain congruence between older adults, who are potential learners, and an educational environment. The intersection where older adults and the learning environment meet can then become growth producing and life-enhancing. By knowing the persons whom we seek to serve—their circumstances, their fears and their dreams—we stand a chance of designing learning opportunities that will enable them to continue becoming who they can be.

Persons in positions to design adult education opportunities could benefit from evaluative comments made by persons in my study.[46] It seemed clear that many persons fifty-five and older have or fear physical limitations. Those seventy and over in particular do not want to go out at night. Meeting locations which require using steps were also seen as detrimental.

Another important factor revolved around leader attitude and competence. Persons who teach older adults need to be sensitive individuals who have some training regarding the biological, psychological, and social needs of older learners. For example, "I can't hear him" and "I can't remember enough of what I learned" illustrate conditions and concerns of which leaders need to take cognizance. Persons who teach older adults need to be accepting and to recognize the cognitive, affective, and lifestyle needs which older learners have. They need to know how to deal with persons who monopolize or otherwise disrupt the learning experience. A need for competence in subject matter, methodological skill, and interpersonal communication skills on the part of leaders of older adults, then, are all important keys to good adult education.

A Model for Adult Learning

Adult education has had many practitioners and few theorists. James Broschart maintains that "we might be well advised to examine 'what works' regardless of its theoretical derivation."[47] Nevertheless, it would be extremely beneficial to the development of an interdisciplinary field of study like adult education to provide a conceptual framework from which to organize research and to begin to develop theory.[48]

Much adult education has been based on a market orientation, which assumes that is you give people what they want, they will "buy" it. A careful critique of this approach has been done by Maurice Monette. He maintains that education can never be value-free and that any theory of adult learning must be explicit about the values being espoused, and then it must be open to critical evaluation by the participants. Monette advocates "double-loop learning" which "involves a critical examination of the assumptions, values, or beliefs underlying the paradigm itself."[49]

Double-looped learning can lead to transformation as persons make a critical appraisal of their basic assumptions and values. It places a high value on pluralism by recognizing that there are alternative ways of perceiving and acting.[50]

Double-looped learning can underlie the development of an adult learning paradigm that is holistic because it recognizes, but does not absolutize, both the felt needs of the learners and the perspective of the educator. It encourages critical thinking on the part of both planner and learner. Indeed, all participants both plan and learn as they struggle with naming and solving the task at hand.

A conceptual framework which might provide a beginning point is to begin with Kurt Lewin's idea of a force field where positive and negative forces are at play against one another.[51] Using an interactive approach, we might diagram our understanding of a contextual approach to adult education as shown on page 69.

To understand how older adults learn, we must begin with the total physical and social environment. To try to explain adult learning apart from the environment will give an incomplete picture at the very least and will probably give a distorted and inaccurate view.

Adults need to be studied as persons in progress through the phases of life, with periods of transition from one phase to another. Each individual may experience crises from time to time. These crises may involve such things as the

Diagram 3.5
A Contextual Model for Adult Learning

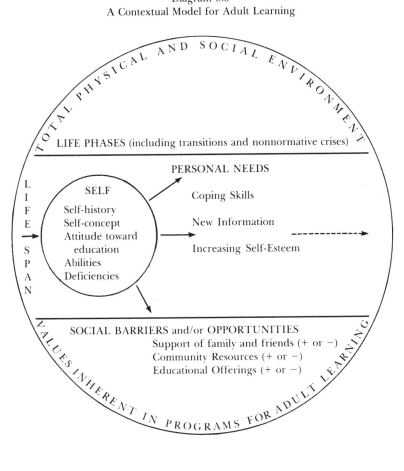

death of a child or a spouse, divorce, serious accidents or illnesses, the loss of one's job, or retirement.

At any given point in one's movement through the life span, an individual is a self. That self has a unique life history which has been shaped, in part, by the historic realities which affect the cohort of which one is a part. The self-concept of any individual is important. It has been shaped by both the biological abilities and deficiencies which one has and the environmental influences which have interacted with them. The potential older adult learner brings who she or he is to the learning experience. That persons have needs, as we have seen when we looked at Abraham Maslow and Erik Erikson, is clear. Those needs include the need for coping skills, for new information of varying types, and for increasing one's self-esteem in order to become more fully what one can be.

The environment brings a wide range of barriers (negative forces) and opportunities (positive forces) to bear on the individual. The actions and reactions of family members and friends can serve to enable or to block learning. Community resources can also serve as either positive or negative factors. For example, public transportation might be readily and economically available, or it might be nonexistent. A given community might support and encourage adult learners, or it might view the need for older adults to engage in learning opportunities as unnecessary and/or remedial. The educational opportunities for older adults might be relevant, accessible, adequately advertised, and low cost; on the other hand, they might not meet the needs of many adults, be expensive, inconveniently scheduled, and/or not well-advertised. Every educational opportunity has certain values inherent in it, and these values—explicit or implicit—are brought to bear on the persons engaged in learning.

It is important to recognize that what might be perceived as a challenge and an opportunity to some adults might be perceived as a threat and a barrier to other adults. For example, a class on "Religions of the World" taught by an articulate and knowledgeable college professor might be a welcome challenge to some well-read or well-traveled persons, but it might be intimidating and threatening to others who have a provincial viewpoint and who believe that theirs is the only true religion.

The diagram above would be more effective if everything on it were in motion—forces and influences and persons and needs—interacting. As persons move through the life span, they seek congruence as they strive to make sense of their life in the world.

Conclusion

That older adults can continue to learn is clear. That older adults face situations which require them to reorganize the ways they experience life is also clear. Education can be a positive resource for "helping persons understand, explore, and enhance the patterns by which they organize their meaning."[52]

Lifelong learning is a prerequisite for survival in the world today. Education for older adults that is relevant, and that addresses the problems and challenges they face, will aid them in being lifelong learners.

Chapter Three Notes

1. Alfred Binet and R. B. Cattell are theorists in the psychometric tradition, and Jean Piaget represents the cognitive tradition. For a more detailed discussion of theoretical models of intelligence see Margaret H. Huyck and William J. Hoyer, *Adult Development and Aging* (Belmont, California: Wadsworth Publishing Company, 1982), pp. 162–194.

2. Huyck and Hoyer, *Adult Development and Aging*, pp. 168–169.

3. J. P. Guilford, *The Nature of Human Intelligence* (New York: McGraw-Hill, 1967).

4. J. L. Horn, "Human Abilities Systems," in P. B. Baltes, ed., *Life-span Development and Behavior*, Vol. 1 (New York: Academic Press, 1978), pp. 211–256. For a comprehensive review of gerontological literature on this topic see K. W. Schaie, "The Primary Mental Abilities in Adulthood: An Exploration in the Development of Psychometric Intelligence," in P. B. Baltes and O. G. Brim, Jr., eds, *Life-span Development and Behavior*, Vol. 2 (New York: Academic Press, 1979).

5. Sherry L. Willis and Paul B. Baltes, "Intelligence in Adulthood and Aging: Contemporary Issues," in Margaret H. Huyck and William J. Hoyer, *Readings In Adult Development and Aging* (Boston: Little, Brown and Company, 1982), p. 207.

6. Lewis R. Aiken, *Later Life*, 2nd ed. (New York: Holt, Rinehart and Winston, 1982), pp. 76–79.

7. Ibid., p. 81. This research was conducted by Baltes and Schaie in 1974.

8. Willis and Baltes, "Intelligence in Adulthood and Aging," pp. 204–207.

9. Aiken, *Later Life*, p. 81.

10. Huyck and Hoyer, *Adult Development and Aging*, pp. 184–187.

11. Willis and Baltes, "Intelligence in Adulthood and Aging," pp. 212–215.

12. Ibid., p. 213. Copyright (1980) by the American Psychological Association. Reprinted by permission of the author.

13. Thomas A. Ringness, *The Affective Domain in Education* (Boston: Little, Brown and Company, 1975), p. 123.

14. Ibid., pp. 122–123.

15. Abraham H. Maslow, *Motivation and Personality* (New York: Harper, 1954), p. 223.

16. Lewis Sherrill, *The Gift of Power* (New York: The Macmillan Company, 1961), p. 83.

17. J. P. Guilford, *Intelligence, Creativity and their Educational Implications* (San Diego: Robert R. Knapp, Publisher, 1968), pp. 81–82.

18. Ibid., pp. 91–96.

19. Ibid., pp. 185–188.

20. Huyck and Hoyer, *Adult Development and Aging*, pp. 190–191.

21. K. Warner Schaie and James Geiwitz, *Adult Development and Aging* (Boston: Little, Brown and Company, 1982), pp. 413–418.

22. J. R. Kidd, *How Adults Learn*, rev. ed. (New York: Association Press, 1973), pp. 36–38.

23. See Malcolm S. Knowles, "Andragogy Revisited Part II," *Adult Education*, Vol. 30, No. 1 (Fall, 1979), pp. 52–53.

24. Malcolm S. Knowles, *The Modern Practice of Adult Education: Andragogy Versus Pedagogy* (New York: Association Press, 1970), pp. 38–39.

25. From Malcolm Knowles, *The Adult Learner: A Neglected Species*, Second Edition. Copyright 1978 by Gulf Publishing Company, Houston, Texas. All rights reserved. Used with permission.

26. For a discussion on Knowles assumptions underlying andragogy, see Leon McKenzie, *The Religious Education of Adults* (Birmingham, Alabama, Religious Education Press, 1982), pp. 120–124.

27. K. Warner Schaie and James Geiwitz, *Adult Development and Aging* (Boston: Little, Brown and Company, 1982), p. 307.

28. From K. Warner Schaie and James Geiwitz, *Adult Development and Aging*. Copyright 1982 by K. Warner Schaie and James Geiwitz. Reprinted by permission of the publisher, Little, Brown and Company.

29. Schaie and Geiwitz, *Adult Development*, p. 312–315.

30. Ibid., p. 316.

31. Ibid., pp. 323–326.

32. Ibid.

33. Robert J. Havighurst, "Education Through the Adult Life Span," *Educational Gerontology*, Vol. 1 (1976), p. 49.

34. Irene Mortenson Burnside, *Working with the Elderly: Group Processes and Techniques* (North Scituate, Massachusetts: Duxbury Press, 1978) p. 90.

35. Walter B. Kolesnik, *Motivation: Understanding and Influencing Human Behavior* (Boston: Allyn and Bacon, 1978).

36. Ibid., p. 146.

37. Roger Boshier, "Educational Participation and Dropout: A Theoretical Model," *Adult Education*, Vol. 23, No. 4 (1973) pp. 255–282.

38. A. H. Maslow, *Motivation and Personality*, 2nd ed. (New York: Harper & Row, 1970) and *Religions, Values and Peak-Experiences* (Columbus: Ohio State University Press, 1964); Carl Rogers, *Freedom to Learn* (Columbus, Ohio: Charles E. Merrill Publishing Company, 1969) and *On Becoming a Person* (Boston: Houghton Mifflin, 1961). Also see John L. Elias and Sharan Merriam's chapter on Humanistic Adult Education in *Philosophical Foundations of Adult Education* (Malabar, Florida: Robert E. Krieger Publishing Co., 1980).

39. Rogers, *On Becoming A Person*, p. 35.

40. Maslow, *Motivation and Personality*, p. 92. Also see A. H. Maslow, "A Theory of Human Motivation" in Harold J. Leavitt and Louis R. Pondy, eds., *Readings in Managerial Psychology*, 2nd edition (Chicago: The University of Chicago Press, 1973), pp. 7–25.

41. Lewis J. Sherrill, *The Gift of Power* (New York: Macmillan, 1961), pp. 14, 19–23.

42. Paul Tillich, *The Courage to Be* (New Haven: Yale University Press, 1952), chapter 2.

43. Arnold J. Toynbee, *A Study of History,* abridged by D. C. Somervell (New York: Oxford University Press, 1947), chapter 19.

44. Sherrill, *The Gift of Power,* pp. 25–43.

45. For discussions of barriers to adult education participation see A. Carp, R. Peterson, and P. Roelfs, "Adult Learning Interests and Experiences," in K. P. Cross, J. R. Valley, and Associates, *Planning Non-Traditional Programs: An Analysis of the Issues for Postsecondary Education* (San Francisco: Jossey-Bass, 1974); also see K. Patricia Cross, *Adults As Learners* (San Francisco: Jossey-Bass, 1981), pp. 97–108.

46. Vogel, "How Older Adults Perceive and Legitimize their Adult Education Participation in Churches and Schools."

47. J. R. Broschart, *Lifelong Learning in the Nation's Third Century: A Synthesis of Selected Manuscripts About the Education of Adults in the United States* (Washington, D.C.: HEW Publication No. [OE] 76-09102, U. S. Government Printing Office, 1977), p. 10.

48. Cross, *Adults As Learners,* pp. 109–131, makes this case and has provided a helpful beginning for such a task by outlining a "Chain-of-Response (COR) Model" on p. 124.

49. M. L. Monette, "Need Assessment: A Critique of Philosophical Assumptions," *Adult Education,* Vol. 29, No. 2 (1979), pp. 83–95. Double-loop learning is designed to develop personal freedom which can lead to the transformation of society. It differs from single-loop learning in that it questions the learning paradigm as it engages in problem-solving. Instead of just seeking an answer to a given question, persons engaged in double-loop learning may decide that the question needs to be changed.

50. See Jack Mezirow, "Perspective Transformation," in *Adult Education,* Vol. XXVIII, No. 2 (1978), pp. 100–110.

51. Kurt Lewin, "Frontiers in Group Dynamics: Concept, Method, and Reality in Social Science," *Human Relations,* Vol. 1 (June, 1949), pp. 5–41.

52. Jack L. Seymour, "Approaches to Christian Education," in Jack L. Seymour and Donald E. Miller, *Contemporary Approaches to Christian Education* (Nashville, Tennessee: Abingdon, 1982), p. 15.

CHAPTER FOUR

A Model for Religious Education with Older Adults

"A passage . . . describes a potentially dangerous shift from one state in life to another. My former state and its values and motives are no longer satisfying; they no longer make sense. Disorientation and confusion can result. Such a passage is, for one who would believe, a potentially sacred time, a "kairos." Experienced initially as disorienting and even debilitating, this time is also one of special opportunity—an extraordinary chance to encounter God and to reorient oneself in more loving and generous directions" (Evelyn and James Whitehead, *Christian Life Patterns,* p. 140).

What Is Religious Education?

James Michael Lee has observed that by its very nature, religious education "pushes back the frontiers of an individual's or a culture's way of knowing, feeling, and living."[1] It deals with issues and questions that make a difference in how one sees oneself and the world.

Why Survive? is the title of a book on aging by Robert Butler. That question causes persons to deal with how they see themselves and the world. There are other vital questions which older adults must resolve. Who am I? Why am I (still) here? What can I contribute? How do I live with the choices—good and bad—that I have made during my lifetime? How can I live with my losses?

All of these questions have psychological, sociological, philosophical, and theological implications. These questions are relational. They help us find our center, our roots, and our sense of belonging. The need to know "who I am" and to feel good about that "I" are issues that can be helpfully examined through religious education.

We previously have defined education as planned learning that involves an interactive process which enables persons to discover meaning and to reconstruct and integrate life experience in order to move toward wholeness. Education differs from learning in that education must be intentional. Alfred North Whitehead believes education must be holistic. He writes, "There is only one subject-matter for education, and that is Life in all its manifestations."[2]

Much has been written about the meaning of religion. Wilfred Cantwell Smith maintains that the word "religion" has had so many different definitions that we would do better to drop it from our vocabulary.[3] Smith prefers to work with the concepts of "tradition" and "faith" rather than with "religion." Nevertheless, he retains the adjective "religious" because it refers to the truth that persons "live religiously" as they "participate in . . . transcendence."[4]

Thomas Groome has defined religious education as an activity that is "a deliberate attending to the transcendent dimensions of life by which a conscious relationship to an ultimate ground of being is promoted and enabled to come to expression."[5]

There are religious educators who hold that one must begin with educational theory; there are others who assert that theology is the primary and foundational source for understanding religious education. My position is that religious education needs to be grounded both in educational theory and in theology.

Harold Burgess has delineated four basic approaches to religious education. The following chart summarizes these approaches.[6] Two of Burgess' approaches, the traditional theological approach and the contemporary theological approach, begin with theology, and that becomes the foundation for religious education.

Randolp Crump Miller has defined theology as "the-truth-about-God-in-relation-to humanity."[7] Those proponents of the contemporary theological theoretical approach seem to be engaged more in doing theology than in formal, cognitive, theological concepts. For example, Lewis Sherrill defines Christian education in relational terms—members of the Christian community "participate in and. . . guide changes which take place in persons in their relationships with God, with the church, with other persons, with the physical world, and with oneself."[8]

The social science theoretical approach, of which James Michael Lee is the chief proponent, asserts that "the basic nature of religious instruction is properly described in terms of the causation of desired learning outcomes."[9] Lee maintains that religious education which is supported by "relevant empirical research" within the framework of the social-science approach is more relevant and is superior to a theological approach.[10]

A possible way out of the long-standing controversy between experience-based education and tradition-based education has been offered by Mary Elizabeth Moore.[11] Her model may provide a bridge between a contemporary theological approach and the social science approach. She offers a "traditioning model of education" in which education within the faith community transmits tradition, enables persons to find and understand meaning in their life experiences, and opens up the possibility of personal, communal, and social transformation. This model seeks to integrate the cognitive, affective, and volitional aspects of life as they manifest themselves in action.[12]

What Is Christian Religious Education?

Some scholars are now using the term "Christian religious education" as they seek to develop a model for religious education that occurs within Christian faith communities. This term acknowledges a community's identity as Christian. At the same time it recognizes that much is shared with and drawn from religious educators in faith communities that are not Christian.[13]

There is no simple answer to the question, "What is Christian religious education?" A task force sponsored by the United Methodist Association of Professors of Christian Education (UMAPCE)[14] spent two years struggling to define the academic discipline of Christian education. The debate continues as to whether Christian religious education is, in fact, a discipline or a field of study which draws on a variety of disciplines.[15] In either case, the metaperspective from which one begins greatly influences and shapes what one understands religious education to be, as well as the language one uses to describe it.

There are a variety of approaches to Christian religious education; each approach focuses on a different goal. That means that any theory evolving out of any one approach will be somewhat different from a theory evolving out of another approach. If one believes theory precedes practice, the reverse would be true. Differing theories would yield different goals, contents, and methodologies. It is my belief that theory both forms and is formed by practice and that it evolves from an interactional process.

A summary of five key approaches to Christian education has been developed by Jack L. Seymour and is included in Table 4.2. Persons interested in pursuing a summary and critique of each of these approaches are encouraged to read *Contemporary Approaches to Christian Education.*[16]

My own approach begins with the one Jack Seymour labels "interpretation."[17] It is an approach that draws on the work of Thomas Groome, Evelyn and James Whitehead, James Smart, and Lewis Sherrill. It grows out of what Howard Burgess categorized as the contemporary theological theoretical approach (Table 4.1). As we have already seen, there are many possible ways one might choose to categorize approaches to Christian religious education. Howard Grimes suggests that Jack Seymour's classification provides a way of looking at theory which incorporates both educational theory and theological perspectives.[18]

Like Howard Grimes,[19] I am eclectic in my approach to Christian religious education. While I begin from an interpretation stance, I seek to be informed by the psychosocial developmentalists and by educational theory and practice. I acknowledge the continual need of both individuals and the faith community for liberation; I see the faith community as the necessary context for religious education.

For me, there are important insights to be found in each approach; no single approach encapsulates the whole Truth. Nevertheless, the perspective from which one begins influences what one does and how one does it. Many of the problems which can be identified in each approach may

Table 4.1
Harold Burgess' Comparative Approaches to Religious Education

	Traditional theological theoretical approach	Social-cultural theoretical approach	Contemporary theological theoretical approach	Social-science theoretical approach
AIM	Communicating of a divine message.	Working construct radicated in present social issues.	Teaching the truth about God so that persons accept Jesus Christ as Lord and live lives of discipleship within the Christian Community.	Living a life characterized by love and service to both God and persons.
CONTENT	An authoritative, biblically and theoretically founded message (lecture/preaching).	All of life's possible experiences as they are enriched, interpreted, and controlled in terms of purposes in harmony with the Christian ideal.	Exploration of the "truth-about-God-in relation-to-man" so that faith content and present experience interrelate.	Religion is the substantive content; instructional practice is the structural content.

TEACHER	Agent who transmits the Christian message.	One who guides growing students into meaningful group experience as together they work for the creation of a new world.	One who represents the whole church and is used by God in the revelationally active process of religious education.	A professional specialist who is able to facilitate religious learning.
STUDENT	Recipient of an authoritative divinely ordained, salvific message.	A product of evolution with the potential to develop the higher tendencies and to participate fully in the "democracy of God."	A child of God and a sinner; a person of worth who is capable of relating with God and others, and of choosing to live a life of love. Takes cognizance of developmental knowledge as it relates to learning.	A whole self and is at the center of the pedagogical act.
ENVIRONMENT	Not integral to religious educational theory; may involve home, school, parish church; apart from the "world."	Significant but largely uncontrollable factor involving all life and all existence.	Holy Spirit as the determinative environmental factor relative to religious education.	Critical component of religious education; a deliberately structured environment to facilitate personal living encounter between learner and Jesus.

(continued)

Table 4.1 (Continued)

	Traditional theological approach	Social-cultural theoretical approach	Contemporary theological theoretical approach	Social-science theoretical approach
EVALUATION	Demonstrable student learning outcomes may not follow immediately. Teacher and content of lesson are focus of evaluation.	The "dollar and person costs" as determined by measuring, evaluating, and testing.	The discovery of what is happening in individual lives reflects Christian truth; day-to-day evaluation of student learning outcomes not crucial.	Behavioral objectives evaluated using scientific evidence which is positive and on-going to assist students in attaining desired goals are assigned a vital role.
ADVOCATES	Josef Jungman Clarence Benson Johannes Hofinger Lois E. LeBar	George Albert Coe William Clayton Bower Ernest J. Chave Sophia Lyon Fahs	Randolph Crump Miller Lewis Sherrill James Smart Gabriel Moran D. Campbell Wyckoff Sara Little Iris Cully Howard Grimes	James Michael Lee

Table 4.2
Contemporary Approaches to Christian Education

	Religious instruction	Faith community	Spiritual development	Liberation	Interpretation
Goals	to transmit Christian religion (understandings and practice)	to build the congregation into a community where persons can encounter the faith and learn its life-style	to enable persons to grow in faith to spiritual maturity	to transform the church and persons for liberation and humanization	to connect Christian perspectives and practices to contemporary experiences
View of Teacher	structurer of a learning environment	priest for the community	spiritual director or sponsor	colleague	guide
View of Learner	learner with developmental and personal needs and interests	person struggling to identify with the Christian community; congregation seeking to be faithful	person moving through stages of development to maturity	both "Christian" persons and groups	person seeking to interpret Christianity and experience

(continued)

Table 4.2 (*Continued*)

	Religious instruction	Faith community	Spiritual development	Liberation	Interpretation
Content	Christian religion	Christian community's faith and life-style	Christian faith	critical reflection on life-style in light of Christian faith	Christian story and present experience
Settings for Learning	primarily formal educational settings	community of faith	person's total life	places where Christians are involved in the world	person's total life
Curriculum	teacher structures the learning environment to enable the learner to acquire Christian religion	priest enables congregation to seek to be faithful and exposes "catechumens" to learning points in the community of faith	spiritual director nurtures a person through significant life crises to grow in faith	persons dialogue about their lives so as to bring to awareness structures of power, alternatives for society, and actions for transformation	guide helps persons understand the meaning of experience in relation to the Christian story

Contribution	serious attention to the application of educational research to the church	increased awareness of the community nature of the Christian church and its educational settings	definition of the ways faith grows in children and adults	concern with the church's mission and involvement in issues of social justice and societal transformation	emphasis placed on discovering relationships among Christian faith, God's present activity, and contemporary experience
Problems	expectation of a higher level of professionalism than may be present in church setting; biased toward more formal educational settings and learning of content	difficulty of intentionally using enculturation structures; apparent assumption that a church community is faithful	difficulty of assessing stages of development; overemphasis on the individual	difficulty of dealing with power and change in the church	difficulty of actually doing theological reflection on experience

be guarded against and compensated for if we remain clear and intentional about our beginning point and how other perspectives can enrich it.

Christian religious education should enable persons to seek "knowledge with understanding and the transformation of persons' actions, beliefs, and values."[20] It is, therefore, holistic and should incorporate every aspect of being human—the cognitive, emotional, volitional, and relational—within the context of the social and political realities of existence.

Thomas Groome defines Christian religious education as "a political activity with pilgrims in time that deliberately and intentionally attends with them to the activity of God in our present, to the Story of the Christian faith community, and to the Vision of God's Kingdom, the seeds of which are already among us."[21] A faith community, then, can be understood as a community that is self-transcendent and self-conscious about its past, present, and future.

My approach to Christian religious education is to begin with theologizing, the reflections of the faith community on its experiences as communicated through its stories, its symbols, its ritual life and its values. Faith communities provide both the context (environment) and the content (story, symbols, rituals, values) of religious education. Methodologies (ways of teaching) should be consistent with a faith community's ultimate commitments as they are reflected in theological assumptions.

For example, if a Christian community affirms that salvation is a gift, its ways of teaching should not communicate that salvation comes through right belief, right action, or right feeling. In a Christian community where it is affirmed that all persons (be they child, youth, young adult, middle-aged adult, or old adult) are loved by God, learners (be they community leaders, criminals, parents, laborers, or professionals) will be valued as persons of worth just as the teacher is. It should be assumed that learners and teachers alike are all equally in need of God's forgiveness and can be made new creatures in Jesus Christ.

Individuals live out their Christian life in a particular faith community that may be United Methodist, Roman Catholic, Baptist, Presbyterian, or . . . That means that they should find appropriate ways of engaging in religious teaching and learning which take into account the perspectives of their own faith community.

For example, a faith community that takes a strong doctrinal position and emphasizes right belief is likely to develop a catechetical approach to teaching/learning. Learners would be encouraged to reappropriate the beliefs of that particular faith community to insure that they come to know and accept those beliefs.

On the other hand, United Methodists would need to be cognizant of the teachings of John Wesley. According to Wesley, faith grows and is to be tested by Scripture, tradition, experience, and reason.[22] Anything that is contrary to any of these guides needs to be questioned by persons in that faith community. There are clearly methodological implications for teachers in a United Methodist faith community. They would violate their students if they were to teach them that to know God all persons must experience God's call in church and respond to an altar call by going forward. That may have been their experience, and they can share it if and when it seems appropriate. But their faith community asserts that there are many avenues to God, and their teaching should reflect that fact.

The point is, the faith community should be intentional about its responsibility for Christian religious education. It provides the context, the content, and at least some parameters for appropriate methodologies. Theological convictions can motivate and impel a faith community toward collective action as it lives, studies, grows, and witnesses.[23]

Theologizing and Christian Religious Education

The theological assumptions of faith communities and of individuals (teachers and students) greatly influence the content and process of Christian religious education. Thomas Groome believes theology informs religious education as it interprets the Story and Vision of the faith community. Christian religious education that is theologically uninformed, Groome asserts, is an aberration.[24]

Theologizing ought not be confused with systematic theology. Persons reflect on their faith experiences in a variety of ways as we have seen. Theologizing involves this reflection in order to express faith in clear and understandable ways.[25]

Mary Elizabeth Moore maintains that a faith community is, in fact, a theologizing community "where historical tradition, contemporary experience, and future hope coexist and exercise their influence."[26] The Bible is an important tool for persons in Christian faith communities who are seeking to find meaning for their lives. Lewis Sherrill maintains that the central purpose for using the Bible in Christian religious education is to enhance the "continuing encounter" with God.[27] Encountering God necessarily involves the whole person. Experience, feelings, and lifestyle must be reflected upon and organized in a meaningful way as persons seek to grow in faith.

What one believes about why and how God confronts and

communicates with persons needs to be understood as one seeks to teach. The content of one's beliefs will vary from one faith community to another. But there will be clear ramifications for Christian religious education which evolve from the assumptions that are made about theological issues. Douglas Wingeier[28] maintains that key theological issues to be considered include revelation, creation, the nature of persons, the nature of the faith community and incarnation. Theologizing might engage one in asking questions such as these.

Revelation

What is revelation? How does God disclose God's power and presence to persons?

One possible answer is that revelation is without meaning until it is perceived. It is God revealing God's self to persons. Revelation is confrontation and meeting. Revelation, like faith, addresses the whole person. Lewis Sherrill suggests that the means of God's self-disclosure include the natural world, persons, events in history, and (for Christians) Jesus Christ who is the living Word of God. The purpose of revelation is redemptive and the context for revelation is the faith community.[29]

Creation

Is God still creating or is creation accomplished? What purpose do persons have in the created order? Are they to be obedient servants to the Creator or are they called to be co-creators?

What one believes about creation will have implications for how one portrays God. Is God unchanging and forever the same or is God responsive to persons and their needs and actually involved in an unfolding creative act? Can God's will be changed? Are persons predestined from the beginning of time or are they created free to choose to say "yes" or "no" to God's call?

The Nature of Persons

Are persons potentially good or are they basically evil? Does being created in the image of God (Genesis 1:26–31) continue to describe who persons really are after the fall (Genesis 3)? What does it mean to say all persons are sinners? What does it mean to say all persons are children of God? Did God create persons for blind obedience or to think and question and assume responsibility for decisions made? From what and for what are persons saved? What is Christian freedom? What is the relationship between discipleship and freedom?

What one believes about the nature of persons and their relationships to other persons and to God will have a profound affect on how one sees one's self as a teacher as well as on how one approaches students.

Nature of the Faith Community

What is the nature of the faith community? Is it called by God and/or created by persons? Is it to minister to its members and/or the world? Is it a voluntary organization or a covenant community? What are the tasks it is intended to perform? What must one do or believe or feel or be to be a part of your faith community?

These questions can be applied to any religious community. They need to be answered by Jews and Christians as they seek to understand their place in their synagogue or church.

Incarnation

A major theological issue that affects all Christian religious education revolves around the question, "Who is Jesus Christ?" How does God make God's self known in the world? Is incarnation, like creation, an event in history; or is it an ongoing experience that continues to manifest itself through the Holy Spirit? What is the meaning of Jesus' birth, life, death, and resurrection?

These questions focus on the very heart of Christian religious education. Implied in them are one's beliefs about the nature of God, persons, and the faith community. Before anyone endeavors to teach those who want to know Jesus, they need to reflect deeply on the questions, "Who is Jesus?" and "What has Jesus to do with me and those I teach?"

Affirmations and Implications: An Example

One response to these questions might be to affirm that "the Word became flesh and dwelt among us" (see John 1:1–14). Jesus was born in Bethlehem and grew up in the home of Mary and Joseph in Nazareth. He was, then, a person, like us, who experienced fully what it means to be human. Jesus opened himself fully to the Spirit of God and entered into a ministry of loving, healing, teaching, and serving all persons—Samaritans and Jews, women and men, lepers and kings. Jesus experienced the joys of being understood and the anguish of being misunderstood. He experienced weariness, anger, compassion, hope, and rejection. Finally, Jesus was betrayed by those he knew best and he suffered an agonizing death on a cross. Jesus was obedient to God's will, as he understood it, in death as well as in life. And God's power proved greater than people's power to silence God's Word. Jesus was raised from the dead. His disciples subsequently were raised from fear and speechlessness (see Luke 22:54–62) to power to proclaim God's victory over sin and death (see Acts 4).

Others, too, can be transformed because Jesus Christ "died for all, that those who live might live no longer for themselves but for him who for their sake died and was raised" (2 Corinthians 5:15). Indeed, the apostle Paul affirmed: "If any one is in Christ, he is a new creation, the old has passed away, behold, the new has come. All this is from God, who through Christ reconciled us to himself and gave us the ministry of reconciliation; that is, God was in Christ reconciling the world to himself, not counting their trespasses against them, and entrusting to us the message of reconciliation" (2 Corinthians 5:17–19).

Central to these affirmations would be the belief that all are forgiven and empowered by God in order to love and forgive the unlovable. All are made new in order to engage in a ministry of reconciliation in a world that is torn by greed and war. All are called to love those whose politics and lifestyle may be offensive, as well as those who share these beliefs. God's incarnate Word lives today and can be shared with others. One way to share it is through Christian religious education.

God may be seen as actively engaged in the ongoing process of creation. Persons may be viewed as being created in God's image—that is, with a capacity to give and receive love and to seek justice and righteousness in order to live in harmony with the created order. All persons—like Eve and Adam—seek to be self-sufficient and, therefore, alienate themselves from self, other persons, and God. There is no way one can save oneself from the traps of self-sufficiency and irresponsibility in a world that engenders greed and selfishness. Therefore, it is only by God's gracious act of forgiving us and receiving us as we are that we can say "yes" to God's gift and be made whole again.

Persons who say "yes" to the Creator find that reconciliation with self, others, and God is a reality. These persons, then, are freed to live and love without fear of death or enslavement to the powers that permeate our world.

All persons have the potential for receiving this gift and living their lives in order "to do justice, and to love kindness, and to walk humbly with . . . God" (Micah 6:8).

The faith community, which is the church for Christians, is called by God to be the "body of Jesus Christ" (e.g., Romans 12:3–8; 1 Corinthians 10: Ephesians 4:4–7). It includes all those who acknowledge Jesus as Lord and is called to witness to God's saving love so that everyone on earth might be made whole. The church is called to serve— "to preach good news to the poor . . . to proclaim release to the captives and recovering of sight to the blind, to set at liberty those who are oppressed, to proclaim the acceptable year of the Lord" (e.g., Luke 4:18–19; also Isaiah 61:1–2).

One cannot follow Jesus Christ without becoming a part of his body, the church. The church, like individuals, sins and falls short of its calling. Even so, God continues to refine, forgive and use the church in the world to bring about God's purpose of love and justice for all.

One who views theological issues in this way engages in Christian religious education in a way quite different from a Jehovah's Witness or a strict Calvinist or a Baptist. Once one has examined and articulated one's basic theological assumptions, it becomes possible to seek an educational methodology that grows out of, and is congruent with, one's beliefs.[30]

Story and Vision for Older Adults

We have already examined the adult life span. It is clear that as persons journey through life they influence and are influenced by their physical and social environment. Their pilgrimage involves meeting and coping with the events and situations that come as they move through the phases of life with their own unique crises and/or marker events and their own opportunities.

One of the opportunities which persons can have is to join others in a pilgrimage of faith as they journey through life. Faith must be seen in comprehensive terms which include believing, trusting, and doing.[31] The pilgrimage can be seen as "faith seeking understanding."[32] Persons engage in a process of interpretation whereby they bring who they are and can become to a community which has a Story and a Vision.

The community—made up of persons who gather for worship and study and scatter to witness and serve—also has an identity and potential for being more faithful to its Story and Vision than it has been and is being. In the interaction between individuals who engage in Christian religious education and their faith community, new meanings emerge and new insights are gained; individuals and communities grow in trusting, in understanding, in doing, and in becoming.

Christian religious education can be a means to enable

persons in general, and older persons in particular, to explore meanings in life. There are questions of integrity (e.g., Erickson) which come with old age. They are questions which, if answers can be found, will give personal meaning and a sense of integrity to the old.

As we have seen, these questions revolve around life and death issues. Why must I (or my loved one) die? What meaning is there in suffering? What use am I now that I cannot work? Can any good come out of the losses I am experiencing? Why am I here?

In the past, persons may have believed that self-esteem was the result of being beautiful or wealthy or powerful. Now in mature old age, these resources are apt to fail us. The Judeo-Christian tradition has a Story and a Vision that affirms the worth of persons apart from how they look or what they do.

That Story and Vision can interact with an individual's story and vision and new meanings of self-worth and self-acceptance may result. The personal sense of integrity that is possible allows persons both *to be* who they are and *to accept* others who may be different. True integrity does not need conformity. There is freedom in integrity.

Christian religious education can provide the context to enable older adults to deal with their emotions and their lifestyles. Numerous feelings relating to losses of health, finances, friends, or spouse may neet to be explored. Relationships with middle-aged children and grandchildren may be concerns persons wish to address. Issues revolving around meaningful work, possible remarriage, and living environments may be relevant. Fears of loss of one's independence, becoming a burden, and senility may need to be examined.

Older persons inevitably face losses of various kinds.

American culture has generally viewed loss as personal failure. However, loss and pain are central to the Christian story. The cross with its pain and suffering and loss can lead to joy and hope in the Resurrection. The Christian tradition affirms that by losing one's life for Christ's sake, real life will be found (see Matthew 10:39). Bringing one's losses to the faith community can provide a context for the discovery of new meanings and a sense of spiritual well-being.

Christian religious education for older adults, then, is the continuation of a life pilgrimage within the context of a faith community. Older adults bring their past (their stories) and their hopes for the future (their visions) to the present. Their stories includes a rich array of experiences—some full of joy and satisfaction, some filled with pain and a sense of inadequacy and loss.

Christian religious education is bringing into dialogue and interaction the stories of persons who make up the faith community, and the Story as it has been preserved and is being lived out by the community of faith. At the same time, the visions of the older adults are engaged by the Vision of the faith community.[33]

Packaged answers and doctrinal affirmations will not do. What older adults need is a road map (e.g., Scripture and tradition) and fellow-pilgrims (others in the faith community of all ages—young, old, peers, teachers, and pastors) who will join them on their journey. Together they will care and love; they will experience pain and sorrow; they will study and grow; they will do and be.

Paul Tournier[34] claims that our culture conditions us to act and think and be in certain ways in order for society to function smoothly. This conditioning to live according to "the American Way of Life" is "an economic and social necessity." Nevertheless, it deprives persons of their imagination, spontaneity, and creativity. So it is that "in youth we must interest ourselves in what we do, in order to become competent; in old age, we can interest ourselves in everything, in order to become more human."[35] Old persons can begin to experience universal, self-giving love as they move beyond particular, selfish love. They can experience the grace granted to persons who find life by letting go of everything (see Matthew 16:24–26).

One of the richest resources of any faith community is the life-experiences of its older members. Too often faith communities, like businesses and families and professions, insist on persons playing games and wearing masks. "Put your best side forward." "Don't let it all hang out!" "What they don't know won't hurt them."

These attitudes toward interpersonal relationships block persons from seeking congruence and achieving integrity. The faith community, especially through small study groups, can provide the arena where persons can dare to be themselves—to bare their souls. There they can look honestly at who they are. They can share their mistakes as well as their successes. They can receive and give acceptance because of the acceptance proclaimed by the Story of the faith community.

Religious education occurs within the context of a faith community. Its content is the interaction between the stories and visions of those who participate and the Story and Vision of the faith community. Its methodology is inherent in the context and content of a given faith community.

The Story and Vision of the Christian community is the good news—the Gospel—of Jesus Christ. It is summed up in John 3:16–17: "For God so loved the world that he gave his only Son, that whoever believes in him shall not perish but have eternal life. For God sent the Son into the world, not to condemn the world, but that the world might be saved through him." God's love is so great that "neither death, nor life, nor angels, nor principalities, nor things present, nor things to come, nor powers, nor height, nor depth, nor anything else in all creation will be able to separate us from the love of God in Christ Jesus our Lord" (Romans 8:38–39).

With that Promise in the Christian Story, no life experience needs to be too horrendous to examine and resolve. No person needs to remain outside the love of God.

There are dangers inherent within Christian communities of faith, however. Because they may have bought into the success orientation of our culture, there may be a temptation to block persons from exposing their stories. There may be a temptation to block persons from asking the hard questions and grappling openly with their doubts and failures. The temptation may be to give easy answers— "Just have faith!" and "Trust God." Because Christians are also members of a culture that deifies self-sufficiency and independence, the temptation is great to produce rather than assuage guilt by saying things like, "He must not have enough faith" or "God must be punishing her for a terrible sin" or "A Christian wouldn't feel like that" or "Christians must never doubt."

Christian religious education occurs at the intersection of persons' life stories and visions with the Story and Vision of the faith community.[36] The environment needs to be open, to promote dialogue, and to accept conflict as both persons and faith communities struggle deeply and honestly with who they are and who they can become. It should value honesty over conformity and persons over doctrines or practices.

Because persons are unique and bring different questions and different needs to a faith community, a variety of educational opportunities needs to be available. Because faith communities differ, the teaching and learning that develops will differ. The teaching/learning in a faith community should enable the meeting of each individual's story and vision with the Story and Vision of that particular faith community.

Christian Religious Education and Older Adults

Older persons come to a particular faith community which embodies certain beliefs and a lifestyle. They bring their own capabilities and needs to educational experiences which seek to enable knowledge, understanding, and transformation.[37]

The following diagram builds on the contextual model for adult learning (Figure 4.3) in order to depict a model for engaging in Christian religious education with older adults.

Older adults are confronted with the need to develop a sense of self-esteem that depends less on being economically productive or on one's social roles. They need to be able to establish and maintain a sense of worth and integrity in spite of biological, psychological, and social losses so that they can acknowledge and interpret the significance of their own lives.

Finally, they must come to terms with and accept the losses of aging and the changes which those losses necessitate.[38]

Evelyn Whitehead has identified six religious images which she believes speak in powerful ways to those who are facing the crisis of integrity vs. despair in later life. They

Figure 4.3
A Model for Christian Religious Education

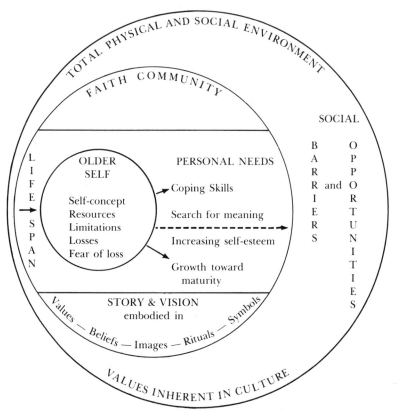

Christian religious education takes place in the lives of older adults when their needs intersect with the Story and Vision of the faith community so that growth in knowledge, understanding and transformation can occur.

include 1) personal salvation, 2) hope, 3) a religious sense of time and personal history, 4) God's unconditional love for the individual, 5) the spiritual discipline of "emptiness" and "letting go," and 6) the image of the Christian as pilgrim-on-the-way.[39]

Once one has accepted the possibility for both personal and social growth throughout the lifespan, "one's experience of change in aging can be interpreted as an invitation from God to continue the process of growth toward full human maturity."[40] The religious images which Evelyn Whitehead lifts up will be powerful images for many older adults in Christian faith communities. For others who may find such images irrelevant, the images may at least point toward "ways in which the imagination of Western civilization has attempted to give expression to its awareness of the potentially positive dimensions of aging."[41]

Case Studies

Case studies can serve as a still photograph of life as it is being experienced by one individual at one time and place. Let us share, briefly, a picture of five persons who are involved in enabling Christian religious education of older adults.

Case Study I: Mr. J

Mr. J has been teaching the class of older adults in Community Church for fifteen years. He is sixty-seven years old and church has been the center of his family's life for as long as he can remember.

Mr. J remembers his grandfather as a big man with a white beard. He was one of the founders of Community Church and his funeral was so big people had to stand outside after the whole church, including the basement, was filled.

Mr. J learned as a boy that God was very powerful and that God knew everything. Even to think bad thoughts was a sin, and you couldn't hide anything from God.

It was important always to go to church, to be strong, and to do the right things. One should always be willing to serve on the church board and to teach Sunday School. If you were a good family man, an upright citizen, and a faithful church member, God would reward you when you died.

Mr. J's class included retired men and their wives, as well as several single women and widows. Mr. J has always taught the uniform lesson series. He resisted attending a curriculum workship to examine new adult resource materials because "studying the Bible was good enough for Grandpa and it's good enough for me."

He prepares diligently for each lesson, using a one-volume commentary and two versions of the Bible as well as the teacher's book. Mr. J does not do too much with suggestions and questions about world issues and politics that may be included in the teacher's book.

"We just stick to the Scripture," he said, "and try to understand what it means to be a righteous man in the eyes of God." Mr. J lectures a great deal, sharing what he learned as he studied the Scripture. Sometimes class members ask a question and once in a while someone shares an idea or an experience that confirms a point Mr. J has made.

Case Study II: Dr. T

Dr. T is a retired professor who taught for forty years. He loves the Scriptures and he loves life. His church school class is made up primarily of couples whose families are grown.

Dr. T grew up in a close-knit family that was involved only marginally in a church community. In college he majored in classics and was greatly influenced by his Greek professor who was a devout Christian. He often was invited to his professor's home and later married the professor's niece.

Dr. T's introduction to Christianity grew out of his experience of acceptance and love by good Christian people who were "on intimate terms with their Savior." He joined a college church where questions were welcomed and differences of opinion were valued and encouraged.

Dr. T said he spent several hours preparing for his church school class each week but "the class almost always ends up going a different direction than I planned."

He said, "I introduce the lesson and we just take off. Someone almost always has a question or wants to tell us about an experience that seems to relate to the topic."

The class has used a variety of resources from curriculum resources focusing on a wide range of topics from "Christian Maturity" to topics like "Why Young People Join Cults." They have to go to the library and research some of their topics rather than having the lesson in a quarterly. Dr. T said they rarely do straight Bible study. Rather, they take topics that interest them, and then he brings in Scripture passages as they seem appropriate.

"Anything we want to study is Christian education," he asserted, "because God is over all and in all and we Christians are doing the studying!"

Case Study III: L. and J. Smith

"We are really facilitators of the Simplified Lifestyle Concerns group in our parish. Our group is committed to personally working toward a simpler lifestyle and to giving support to each other as we all try, in our own ways, to consume less and to live more in harmony with our world," J. said.

Her husband added, "We believe that God's good creation is to be cared for and not exploited." The group studies Scripture and theological writers who address issues which relate to lifestyle. It works together—in the food co-op it organized. It provides opportunities for sharing possible ways of changing one's living patterns and of the feelings which people have about simplifying lifestyles. The group also works in the political arena to support legislation which encourages conservation and improved environmental quality.

The group is intergenerational. J. said, "Our older members have really helped us. They know how to do things that some of us have never experienced."

Case Study IV: M. T.

"I helped organize this ecumenical support group for divorced women with grown children. It's hard to deal with the feelings of guilt and failure that often surface when one's marriage ends after twenty-five or thirty years. Then there may be a deep-seated feeling that God is judging me, too." The group believes that older women have special needs that may be different from younger divorcees.

This group meets weekly to share feelings, to provide support, and to solve problems which arise as these women strive to rebuild their lives. The primary need the participants find being met is emotional. But one woman said, "I have also grown spiritually. For the first time, I know what God's love and forgiveness really is!" Another participant pointed out that learning how to fix a leaky faucet might seem like a small thing; in her case, however, it was a step toward independence.

Experiencing care, finding acceptance, and being challenged to grow were the primary outcomes of this ecumenical group.

Case Study V: Mrs. B

Mrs. B was a seventy-year-old wife, mother, and grandmother who taught her church's Philathia Class, which consisted of two single sisters and seventeen widows. She was hesitant to accept the teaching assignment even though she had been a diligent Bible student all her life.

Mrs. B told me she had wanted to be a mathematics teacher, but her father would not allow her to attend high school because "God intended that women should be wives and mothers."

She married a farmer when she turned seventeen, and they had their first child on her eighteenth birthday. She and her husband attended church regularly, and her husband became a deacon. He always spoke for his family, and she believed the Bible taught that women should keep silent in church.

"I agreed to teach the Philathias because it's only women." They study the Bible, and it is one of the happiest experiences of her life. She reads the passage over at least once a day during the week before they study it. She also reads *Haley's Bible Handbook*. Then she prays over the Scripture and prays for each one of the ladies in her class.

"We read a verse and then we talk about what it means to us. If it seems to go against what I know is right, I ask our pastor about it so I can tell the ladies the next week."

"You know," she said, "my class is growing." They care

about each other and try to help out if anyone has a problem. Her students listen to her and that makes her feel good. "They think I should have been a teacher," she said. "I really do like teaching God's word."

Reflection

These persons bring their own unique experiences to educational ministry in the church. We can begin to see that how and what persons teach are greatly influenced by their past experiences. Their beliefs about who they are and who God is are embodied in their teaching ministry.

Conclusion

We live in a pluralistic culture where there is a wide range of faith perspectives. These range from dogmatic claims to have the whole truth to dogmatic claims that exclude the possibility of faith.

We live in a youth-oriented culture that emphasizes the negative aspects of aging like "pain, suffering, loneliness, and isolation." It tends to ignore the positive aspects of aging like "a growing self-encounter, a greater and deeper expansion of our relationships with other persons and the growing encounter with our God."[42]

The challenge which faces faith communities as they seek to engage in Christian religious education with older adults, and with others as they seek to understand aging, is twofold. One is to counteract the negativity associated with aging; the second is to provide possibilities for persons to maximize the opportunities to widen their horizons, to find meaning in life, and to experience a sense of integrity and wholeness. Whatever theological assumptions one makes and whatever approach one takes to religious education, persons can assume with Bollinger that "the spiritual needs of the aging really are those of every person, writ large: the need for identity, meaning, love and wisdom."[43] Whatever images one chooses to use, faith communities can enable persons to grow in faith, in understanding, and in discipleship.

Chapter Four Notes

1. James Michael Lee, ed., *The Religious Education We Need: Toward the Renewal of Christian Education* (Birmingham, Alabama: Religious Education Press, 1977), p. 119.

2. Alfred North Whitehead, *The Aims of Education and other Essays* (New York: Macmillan, 1959), p. 10.

3. Wilfred Cantwell Smith, *The Meaning and End of Religion* (New York: Mentor Books, 1964), pp. 175–176.

4. Ibid., p. 176.

5. Thomas H. Groome, *Christian Religious Education: Sharing Our Story and Vision* (San Francisco: Harper & Row, 1980), p. 22.

6. The following chart has been developed by Vogel to summarize Harold William Burgess, *An Invitation to Religious Education* (Birmingham, Alabama: Religious Education Press, 1975).

7. Randoph Crump Miller, *The Theory of Christian Education Practice* (Birmingham, Alabama: Religious Education Press, 1980), p. 156.

8. Lewis Sherrill, *The Gift of Power* (New York: Macmillan, 1961), p. 82.

9. James Michael Lee, "The Authentic Source of Religious Instruction," in Norma H. Thompson, ed., *Religious Education and Theology* (Birmingham, Alabama: Religious Education Press, 1982), p. 127.

10. James Michael Lee, *The Shape of Religious Instruction* (Birmingham, Alabama: Religious Education Press, 1971), pp. 311–313.

11. Mary Elizabeth Moore, *Education for Continuity and Change: A New Model for Christian Education* (Nashville, Tennessee: Abingdon, 1983).

12. Ibid., pp. 121–146.

13. For key examples, see Thomas Groome, *Christian Religious Educa-*

tion, pp. 23–26; also see Mary Elizabeth Moore, *Education for Continuity and Change,* p. 9.

14. The United Methodist Association of Professors of Christian Education task force included Allen J. Moore, D. Bruce Roberts, Nelle G. Slater, and Linda Jane Vogel. Its findings and background papers are available from The Division of Education of the Board of Discipleship of the United Methodist Church.

15. For example, Howard Grimes asserts that religious education is a discipline while James Michael Lee believes it must be viewed as a field of study. John Westerhoff III claims that it is "A Discipline in Crisis" (*Religious Education,* Vol. LXXIV, No. 1 [January-February, 1979]), pp. 7–15.

16. Jack L. Seymour and Donald E. Miller, *Contemporary Approaches to Christian Education* (Nashville, Tennessee: Abingdon, 1982). Permission to use this table was granted by Abingdon Press and Chicago Theological Seminary.

17. Jack L. Seymour and Carol A. Wehrheim, "Faith Seeking Understanding: Interpretation as a Task of Christian Education" in Seymour and Miller, *Contemporary Approaches to Christian Education,* pp. 123–143.

18. Howard Grimes, "How I Became What I am as a Christian Religious Educator," in Marlene Mayr, ed., *Modern Masters of Religious Education* (Birmingham, Alabama: Religious Education Press, 1983), p. 153.

19. Ibid., pp. 135–159.

20. Moore, *Education for Continuity and Change,* p. 132.

21. Groome, *Christian Religious Education,* p. 25.

22. The Division of Education, Board of Discipleship, The United Methodist Church, *Foundations for Teaching and Learning in the United Methodist Church* (Nashville, Tennessee: Discipleship Resources, 1979), pp. 23–31.

23. The fact that theology informs collective social action of faith communities is dramatically demonstrated by Paul M. Harrison's study of the American Baptist Convention in *Authority and Power in the Free Church Tradition* (Princeton, New Jersey: Princeton University Press, 1959).

24. Groome, *Christian Religious Education,* pp. 228, 232.

25. John Macquarrie, *Principles of Christian Theology* (New York: Charles Scribner's Sons, 1977), p. 1.

26. Moore, *Education for Continuity and Change,* p. 68.

27. Sherrill, *The Gift of Power,* p. 95.

28. Douglas E. Wingeier, "Principles of Adult Learning and their Implications for Continuing Education for Ministry," Unpublished paper (Naperville, Illinois: Garrett Evangelical Theological School, n.d.).

29. Sherrill, *The Gift of Power,* pp. 69–79.

30. Howard Grimes, "Theological Foundations for Christian Education," in Marvin J. Taylor, ed., *An Introduction to Christian Education* (Nashville, Tennessee: Abingdon, 1966), pp. 32–41.

31. Groome, *Christian Religious Education*, pp. 57–66.

32. Seymour and Wehrheim, "Faith Seeking Understanding."

33. My understanding of religious education has been greatly influenced by Thomas Groome's careful explication of "shared praxis" in *Christian Religious Education: Sharing Our Story and Vision* (San Francisco: Harper & Row, 1980). Other books which have contributed significantly to the development of this section include Evelyn Eaton Whitehead and James D. Whitehead, *Christian Life Patterns: The Psychological Challenges and Religious Invitations of Adult Life* (Garden City, New York: Doubleday, 1979); Lewis Sherrill, *The Gift of Power* (New York: The Macmillan Company, 1961); John H. Westerhoff and Gwen K. Neville, *Generation to Generation* (Philadelphia: United Church Press, 1974).

34. Paul Tournier, *Learn to Grow Old* (New York: Harper & Row, 1971), chapter V.

35. Ibid., p. 212.

36. See Moore's description of teaching in relation to persons at the intersection in *Education for Continuity and Change*, pp. 162–166.

37. Mary Elizabeth Moore makes the case in *Education for Continuity and Change* that educational aims often have tended to separate knowledge, understanding, and transformation. She asserts that the three are so intricately interwoven that such attempts to view them separately may be detrimental to understanding Christian religious education (pp. 152–155).

38. Evelyn Eaton Whitehead, "Religious Images of Aging: An Examination of Themes in Contemporary Christian Thought," in Carol LeFevre and Perry LeFevre, *Aging and the Human Spirit* (Chicago: Exploration Press, 1981), pp. 56–67.

39. Ibid., pp. 64–66.

40. Ibid., p. 63.

41. Ibid., p. 65.

42. Charles E. Curran, "Aging: A Theological Perspective," in Carol LeFevre and Perry LeFevre, *Aging and the Human Spirit* (Chicago: Exploration Press, 1981), pp. 68–82.

43. Quoted by David O. Moberg, "Spiritual Well-Being: Background and Issues for the Technical Committee on Spiritual Well-Being," *1971 White House Conference on Aging* (Washington, D.C.: U. S. Government Printing Office, 1971), p. 1.

CHAPTER FIVE

Teaching Older Adults

"Do not cast me off in the time of old age;
forsake me not when my strength is spent.
For my enemies speak concerning me,
   those who watch for my life consult together,
   and say,
'God has forsaken him; pursue and seize him,
   for there is none to deliver him'"
(Psalm 71:9–11).

Health, the level of education persons have achieved, and individual differences are more important factors than is age in determining older adults' ability and interest for lifelong learning. Older persons can and do learn. The declines in intellectual ability which have been associated with age are now believed to be associated with the nearness of death rather than with aging as such.[1]

Even with failing health, many older adults can benefit from and enjoy learning opportunities. What and how we teach must be relevant and appropriate for older adult learners.

PLM Teaching-Learning Model

A helpful teaching-learning model which can be applied to our contextual model for adult learning is Howard Mc-

Clusky's PLM Teaching-Learning Model.[2] According to this theory, the relationship between power, "P," (the resources individuals have at their disposal) over the load, "L," (the internal and external demands being made on individuals) equals margin, "M," (the personal capacity and energy available to engage in learning). Thus:

$$\frac{POWER}{LOAD} = MARGIN$$

McClusky states that in our rapidly changing world, learning is a prerequisite for survival. What and how persons learn depends on where the person is in their life span, what potential and handicaps for learning exist, as well as on the appropriateness and relevance of the learning opportunity. He believes "the strategies for learning [and for teaching] in the adult years require consideration for the individuality of adults, for their life commitments which may aid or obstruct learning, for their adult time perspective, for their transition through critical periods of life, for their acquired sets and roles which may aid or obstruct learning, and for their adult requirement that the learning be relevant to their problems."[3]

Figure 5.1 shows Keith Main's diagram of the PLM Teaching-Learning Model.

The diagram illustrates that teaching-learning is influenced both by indirect values that are nurturing in nature and by direct, instructional values. It is clear that those who plan for and teach older adults need to give attention to values that affect the teaching-learning process indirectly as well as to those values that have a direct influence.

One of the reasons interest surveys in adult education have not been good enrollment predictors[4] may be ex-

Figure 5.1[5]
Summary of the Teaching-Learning Model

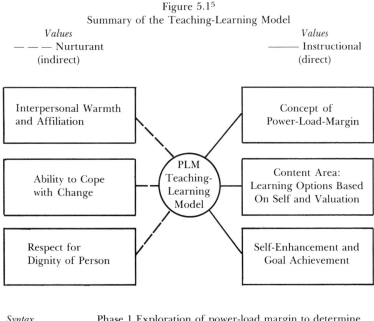

Values	*Values*
— — — Nurturant	——— Instructional
(indirect)	(direct)

Interpersonal Warmth and Affiliation	Concept of Power-Load-Margin
Ability to Cope with Change	Content Area: Learning Options Based On Self and Valuation
Respect for Dignity of Person	Self-Enhancement and Goal Achievement

PLM Teaching-Learning Model

Syntax	Phase 1 Exploration of power-load margin to determine "working margin"
	Phase 2 Clarification of basic value set and self-hood
	Phase 3 Determination of direction and specific learning options
	Phase 4 Implementation of educational objectives and program
Principles of Reaction:	The model encourages mutual respect and shared responsibility. Educational agent is a facilitator and resource person. The learner determines the educational objectives to be achieved.
Social System:	Moderate structure. Fosters spirit of mutual inquiry in small groups or tailor-made learning situations.
Support System:	Margin and motivation for learning a prerequisite. A trained adult educator/facilitator is needed. Environment must be able to respond to a variety of learner demands.

plained by the PLM model. Expressing interest without asking persons to consider how much margin they have, indicates interest but gives little or no indication of their ability or willingness to actually enroll. Teaching adults necessitates being attentive to the resources available to persons, the demands being made on them, and thus, to the margin they have to invest in learning.

Teachers of Older Adults

The effective teacher of older adults can be described first and foremost as an enabler.[6] The teacher as enabler seeks *to authorize* older adults by encouraging them to pursue their interests and aspirations to grow and develop, *to free* them to learn by providing relational support, and *to empower* them by affirming their abilities to achieve their aspirations.

This approach to teaching-learning is illustrated by Thomas Merton when he described Mark Van Doren's teaching. He was not simply passing his thoughts on to his students; rather, he had the ability to share his own vital excitement and interest in things as well as some things about his approach to learning. What resulted was not always predictable. He sometimes was surprised and learned things his students had discovered that he, himself, had not yet forseen.[7]

In order to be an enabler, one must have competencies in interpersonal and nurturing skills. One must be secure with who one is, and be clear about one's own values. Then the enabler can relate to older adult learners as they are and help them clarify their own goals and values (which need *not* be the same as the enabler's). An enabler knows that both enabler and enablee are equally important. The interaction that occurs is one that encourages both persons to see through the eyes of the other. It is open, honest, and affirming. Adult learners may, in fact, be looking for a caring person with good communication skills and the ability to be their friend and build up their self-esteem, rather than for a "master craftsman."[8]

Three groups of adult learners[9] were asked to describe the "best teachers" they had had. While the lists were varied, some important threads ran through the three lists.

Teachers described as "the best" are interested in those they teach as unique persons. They are perceptive, empathetic and are attentive listeners. These teachers are knowledgeable about what they teach, are organized, and are well prepared. At the same time, they are open to and accepting of differing opinions. They are flexible and are able to motivate students to learn on their own.

These persons care about the world and are knowledgeable about a wide variety of subjects beyond their teaching area. They are open-minded, honest, and have a sense of humor. They exhibit self-respect and are committed to learning as well as to teaching.

Harry Overstreet maintains that a teacher of adults must, first of all, be a learner. At the same time, an effective teacher must have expertise in the matter being taught and have a sense of the larger picture that goes beyond narrow specialization. Finally, a teacher must be able to experience and nurture a sense of community as she or he relates to persons in the world.[10]

There are skills and abilities which teachers of older adults need.[11]

It is crucial that teachers of older adults have an understanding of, and respect for, the learners they teach. This includes acknowledging the rich resources through life experience and/or education that the learners bring to the teaching-learning experience. It also includes an awareness of the physical limitations and the external pressures which persons bring.

The skill to encourage all persons to participate fully is also important. This necessitates being sensitive to each person and their unique needs as well as to the needs of older adults in general.

Teachers of older adults need expertise in planning an environment that is nonthreatening, comfortable, and conducive to learning. We will examine what is involved in developing such a learning environment in the next section of this chapter.

Teachers of older adults need to have the skills to enable participants to share in setting goals. They need to be able to organize, facilitate, and evaluate the learning experience.

The ability to select appropriate methods and to use a wide variety of methods is also important. No method is so effective that it should be used all of the time. Selecting appropriate methodologies will be dealt with later in this chapter.

To summarize, effective teachers of older adults should be clear about their own self-concept and their own values. They should be knowledgeable about what they teach and have the skills of an enabler. They should be aware of and sensitive to the needs and potentials of those they seek to teach.

In addition, persons who seek to be religious educators should be a part of a faith community which provides the context for learning. They should be clear about the theological foundation out of which they teach.

It is important to note, however, that this does *not* mean that to be a teacher one must have all of the answers. Students and teachers alike are pilgrims on a journey of faith. Educational ministry enables all persons to theologize as they both live out and reflect on their faith. Mary Elizabeth Moore helps us understand the comprehensive nature of that theologizing when she asserts that dealing with our faith necessitates exploring and examining "beliefs, attitudes, commitments and practices."[12]

Planning Learning Experiences

"The key to learning is engagement," according to J. R. Kidd. Learning is relational. The learner, the task or content, the environment, and the enabler must interact to facilitate growth and learning.[13]

Planning for engagement and interaction should begin by reviewing our contextual model for adult learning (chapter III). Once we have familiarized ourselves with who we will teach, their physical and social environments, and the social barriers and opportunities which have an impact on the situation, we are ready to assess the values that are inherent in the teaching-learning situation which we are planning.

What assumptions are we making? Why are we teaching? What do we believe about the persons we will teach? What do we believe about the task or content on which we will be focusing? What are our goals? Are they consistent with the goals of the students?

Maurice Monette believes that educational planning should begin with the educators working in cooperation with the community to be served, to determine "a direction for inquiry through a commitment to chosen values within a given socio-cultural context" and "the nature of the educational transaction."[14]

Christian religious education often begins with seeking to transmit the community of faith's Story—its past—to new members. This often takes a form that some might label indoctrination. Whatever we call it, it is vital to the ongoing nature of the community.[15] But Christian religious education should go beyond transmission; it should be explicit about the values that are being espoused, and it should encourage critical thinking about those values and the educational process on the part of each participant.[16] It should address the tasks of both transmission and transformation.

It is important to identify a problem, need, or area to be explored. What is it that persons hope will result? For example, do they want to gain more information, to develop a skill, or to participate in a stimulating experience?

Next it is important to examine possible ways to achieve the desired result. Once options have been examined, the persons involved in planning can decide on the most appropriate and feasible courses of action. In working with older adults, the following guidelines are helpful.[17]

1) *Select options which make use of the older learners' life experiences.* One of the richest resources for learning is the many and varied experiences which older learners have had. Studies show that learning is enhanced when it grows out of and builds upon the life experiences of the learners.

2) *Make use of mental pictures and images in order to aid persons in making associations.* Retention is improved when persons are able to relate new information and ideas to past experiences and knowledge. Helping older persons learn by using mental pictures and images can improve their ability to deal with abstract concepts.

3) *Encourage self-pacing.* This is much better than options which put persons under pressure to respond or to keep up with others. There is much less variance between the young and old in their ability to learn when time is not a factor. Older persons may require more time to learn. Given adequate time, older persons can and do learn.

4. *Provide clearly focused attention on the learning task or topic.* This will enable persons to overcome their increased susceptibility to distraction. Being sure that extraneous noise is eliminated is also important.

5) *Emphasize verbal abilities.* There is evidence that, in older adults, verbal abilities are the least susceptible to decline. Teachers can make use of and enhance verbal abilities by speaking slowly and distinctly. Facing one's listeners when one speaks is also an important aid in facilitating learning.

6) *Emphasize practical applications for new learning.* Older adults generally prefer learning settings where they can be involved and can actively participate in the learning. Then they want to be able to use what is learned. Problem-centered learning is valued by most older learners.

In planning with and for older adults, it is crucial to remember that the life history persons bring to the teaching-learning experience greatly colors the way persons perceive. Those past experiences may block, modify, or aid persons in the learning process.[18]

Robert Havighurst builds on this understanding when he emphasizes the "teachable moment" and the need to capitalize on issues relating to the developmental learning tasks when they are of primary concern to individuals. He identifies the following learning tasks for older adults: 1) to adjust to having less physical strength and decreasing health, 2) to adjust to retirement and reduced income, 3) to adjust to the death of one's spouse, 4) to establish an explicit affiliation with one's own cohort, 5) to adapt to changing social roles, and 6) to establish satisfactory physical living arrangements.[19]

Persons learn best when they need or want something. Providing the opportunity to gain new knowledge, new skills, or to broaden one's experience at a time when persons are ready and open to such learning is a key.

Research has shown that changing roles call for adaptation. This can lead persons to seek education as a means of making the necessary adaptations.[20] Some possible "teachable moments" for older adults, then, may include finding a new focus when one's children leave home, adjusting to a changing relationship with one's very old parents, facing retirement and increased leisure, and adapting to the loss of one's spouse and/or one's health and independence.

For example, preretirement education might be just what is needed by a group of sixty-year-olds who are facing what life will be like when they leave the work force. An opportunity to experiment with a new hobby may be the stimulation some older persons want once they are settled in a small apartment in a retirement complex and no longer have a large home and yard to care for. Classes in painting or German may meet their needs.

Planning needs to cover the very basic and mundane as well as the philosophical. In addition to what and how, planners need to determine when and where the learning opportunity will take place. Wonderfully conceived and relevant plans have been known to fail because the when and where were inappropriate for the audience for which they were planned.

Selecting resources—including printed materials, field trips and human resources—is an important part of the planning process. This is an area where the teacher's expertise is vitally important. Serving as a resource person is an important enabling task. One need not have all the answers, but it is important to know where and how to find them.

Evaluation is an integral part of any educational endeavor and it needs to be included in the planning process. Evaluation will be discussed in greater detail later in this chapter.

It should be clear by now that our approach to planning teaching-learning experiences is not limited to a Tylerian approach to learning which focuses around 1)purpose, 2) experiences to attain the purpose, 3) organization of those experiences, and 4) evaluation.[21] Rather, we begin with an examination of values being espoused and then seek to develop a "double-loop learning" situation which includes critical thinking about both our value presuppositions and the educative process. There are fewer givens and greater flexibility in this approach.

It acknowledges that adult educators must move beyond a service orientation which only examines and responds to the felt-needs of learners within a predetermined framework. Rather, adult education must enable learners to move beyond the technical mode of valuing toward acceptance of responsibility for paradigm-shifting and tranforming the social system in ways that promote increased freedom and autonomy for all persons. This kind of teaching-learning calls for critical thinking about underlying values and assumptions as well as about the ways one seeks to learn and grow.[22] It is an interactive approach which seeks to foster self-responsibility and a process of becoming for each participant.

When the learning being planned is Christian religious education, the faith community provides the context, and the theological perspective of that community provides the basis from which to explore issues. Context and content provide parameters for selecting appropriate methodologies. Evaluation must include self-evaluation and generally involves assessing one's growth toward wholeness.

Structuring a Learning Environment

The learning environment includes both the social/emotional environment and the physical environment.[23] Of the two, the social environment is most crucial.

An environment that is conducive to older adults learning, needs to be inviting and to communicate support and acceptance. It should be nonthreatening.

The learning environment includes both the physical and the psychosocial climate where learning takes place. Leon McKenzie includes the following components for an ideal climate for the teaching-learning of adults: "1) the physical comfort of the learners, 2) freedom of expression, 3) mutual trust and respect, and 4) shared responsibility for learning activities and outcomes."[24]

The environment should not be created apart from the persons for whom it is being designed. For example, a very intimate setting with soft chairs in a close circle might be threatening to some older persons and very inviting to others.

I went into a church-school classroom that had upholstered chairs with wooden arms lined up in three straight rows. A small table was in the front of the room. A straight-backed chair was behind the table facing the rows of chairs. A set of Bible maps was beside the small table.

My initial reaction to the room was that it would not be

conducive to fostering interaction. I would have liked to put the chairs in a circle, or at least a semi-circle.

The older adults that meet in this little room off to the side of the sanctuary have been together as a class for forty years. Many are widowed now. They range in age from fifty-eight (a young wife) to ninety-four. The mean age is seventy-three. Their teacher, a seventy-nine-year-old retired professor, has taught the class for twenty years. He spends much time studying the lesson and then uses a lecture approach in teaching. The class members are very satisfied with the way things are. When the teacher had a stroke and was unable to teach, they decided to disband temporarily since the winter weather made it difficult to attend anyway. Now the teacher and the students are back, and I will be the first to admit that theirs is a warm and comfortable social environment.

My adult church-school class was once the young-married class. Now some of us have grandchildren, and there are two adult classes "below us"! Our room is under the eaves—two flights of stairs above the sanctuary. We have an old sofa and two over-stuffed chairs (you have to arrive early to get them) as well as about twenty folding chairs. All of the chairs are lined up along the walls. The focal point is a small table with hot water for coffee and tea and some baked goodies.

The leader, who may be any one of a half dozen class members depending on the topic and who volunteered, generally sits on one of the chairs near a blackboard that is mounted on the wall. Discussion is the usual format and no leader can carry on very long without losing the floor.

Neither classroom I have described would be chosen to illustrate a text book on creating learning environments. Both of them could be improved in a number of ways.

Nevertheless, the social environment in both classes is an accurate reflection of the personalities of the classes involved. Their social environments are appropriate. This leads me to conclude that both groups create and are created by their environment. The relationship between a group or class and its setting is interactive. Each will be affected by the other.

It is possible, then, to create environments in order to be manipulative. There is a narrow line between enhancing learning by creating a growth-producing environment (which can be done and is positive) and creating an environment in order to achieve the teacher's goals (which can be destructive if it violates the identity of the group).

A key to creating a social environment for older adults is that it is the responsibility of the entire group. Group decisions ought to be encouraged. The goals of the group ought to provide the framework for creating the setting. Experimentation might be encouraged.

For example, someone might ask the members of the oldest class whether they might hear better if the chairs were in a semicircle around the teacher's table. They might or might not decide to try it. If they did, it would be their decision and their social environment would not have been violated. If they are more comfortable with things the way they have always been, so be it.

There are things that can be done to enhance the physical environment to enable older adults to learn. Even so, one must remain cognizant of how improving the *physical* environment might be perceived as destroying the *social* environment.

Some factors should be remembered, however. Nearly everyone over age sixty has some disability or disease. Forty percent of all persons sixty-five or over have some chronic condition which places limitations on their level of activity.[25] Common problems include arthritis, heart disease, hypertension and diabetes. Sensory losses—especially seeing and hearing—become more noticeable as people age.

The necessity of climbing steps can be a hindrance to participation of older adults. Firm, straight-backed chairs are often preferred because they are easier to get out of.

A lack of disruptions including background noises, bright light, and excessive breezes (drafts) is conducive to learning. Good acoustics and clearly marked rooms (meeting rooms, restrooms, etc.) are important. Visual aids that use large lettering can supplement verbal instructions.

Having a space to "own" is very beneficial, though it is not always possible. If a group cannot have a room to call its own, a portable bulletin board where displays can be stored and then put out intact may help persons to feel like they belong.

Again, involving participants in creating their own physical environment can yield good results. Such activities may build a sense of community. Persons who know that their contributions are important often feel commitment to the group. Attention needs to be given to the social and physical learning environments. Removing physical barriers and creating an appropriate physical setting without disrupting the social environment can enhance the learning of older adults.

Selecting Appropriate Methodologies

We will use the term "methodologies" to mean those approaches and strategies selected as means to achieve our educational goals. Discovery methodologies can involve older learners in carefully exploring alternatives as they seek to find solutions to problems. These strategies may generate cognitive, affective, and normative responses.

Persons may engage in a cognitive process, thinking analytically about a problem. Benjamin Bloom has edited a taxonomy of educational objectives which can provide a framework for analytical thinking. It shows that learners move from lower mental processes to higher mental processes. Such movement includes 1) knowledge, 2) comprehension, 3) application, 4) analysis, 5) synthesis, and 6) evaluation.[26]

Analytical thinking involves isolating and defining a problem, and then developing and testing hypotheses in order to draw generalizations or conclusions that are valid and reliable.

Creativity grows out of divergent thinking.[27] It involves a wide range of responses which may not be directly related to evidence or the stimuli at hand. Humor and a willingness to consider possibilities that go beyond conventionality and stereotypic views seem to be characteristic of creative thinking.[28] Many now maintain that "self-actualizing creativeness" is a potential all persons possess and that it can be enabled and nurtured.[29]

Religious education often involves questions focusing on values. David Krathwohl, Benjamin Bloom, and Bertram Masia provide us with a taxonomy which may aid us in understanding educational objectives in the affective domain. They hold that persons internalize values by 1) receiving, 2) responding, 3) valuing, 4) organization, and 5) characterization by a value or value complex.[30] The highest level here presupposes that one has reached a point where one has been able to generalize and to live out one's philosophy of life.

Once again, interaction is the key. Only when one knows

the learners who will participate, the potentials and limitations inherent in the setting where the learning will occur, the abilities and limitations of the teacher, and the purpose and goals of the group, is one in a position to select the methodologies that can most effectively enable persons to learn.

The case has already been made that the context and content of a given learning community sets methodological parameters. For example, in a community that values the intrinsic worth of all persons, competitive methods that promote winning at another's expense would be inappropriate. In a faith community that accepted a certain interpretation of Scripture as the infallible word of God (e.g., creationism), a method that encouraged dissenting points of view would be considered inappropriate.

Once the parameters have been established, a variety of questions need to be examined:

What are the likes and dislikes of the participants? What are their needs and wants? What are their abilities and limitations?

What skills does the teacher possess? What are the limitations due to the setting and teaching resources?

What is it we want to accomplish? What do we want to be able to do and/or to know as a result of this study? What experiences do persons want to have? What attitudes and issues which affect lifestyle choices do persons want to explore?

Given our answers to these questions, what methods might we choose? Once several options have been determined, another list of questions needs to be examined.

Is the time and/or money required to use a given method justifiable? For example, one way to study the Gospel of Matthew would be to use the film, "The Gospel According to St. Matthew." Is the rental fee feasible given the size and resources of your group? Another approach would be to study the book by discussing it verse-by-verse. Since you know that your class averages about ten verses a week when you use this approach, you need to determine if you are willing to spend 107 weeks (over two years) studying the Gospel of Matthew.

Does a particular method maximize the people-resources within your group? For example, if you are doing Bible study, do those who have completed the Bethel Bible Study series have an opportunity to share? Is it growth-producing for the group and for individuals to import leaders on a regular basis if you have retired persons with time and abilities to share?

Variety is a good thing—it can provide spice to life! No single method is appropriate in every situation. Selecting the best method for each situation is a skill that needs to be developed.

Some Guidelines

Lecture is an appropriate methodology when one person is an effective communicator and has information which the entire group needs or wants. Its primary use is to share information, though it can be used to inspire and motivate persons to action.

Discussion is an appropriate methodology when persons have knowledge and/or life experiences which can contribute to achieving the group's goal. Discussion must be more than the sharing of uninformed opinions. It needs to be focused and to move toward resolution of an issue.

Media presentations (films, film strips, tapes, records) can enhance learning if they address the issues the group is working on. They need to be clearly audible, and/or easy to see. Unusual accents or persons who speak rapidly tend to create serious problems for older persons. Relying on only one sense (hearing) is not a good idea since many older persons compensate for hearing deficiencies by relying on lip reading or other visual aids.

Storytelling is a powerful means of communicating with persons of all ages and stages, and it ought not be overlooked as an effective methodology by and for older adults. It must be relevant to the learning goals of the group.

Demonstrations can be effective. This is especially useful for older persons who may have difficulty dealing with abstractions or complicated instructions that are given verbally. Care must be taken to see that everyone can see and the pace of the demonstration may need to be slowed down.

Hands-on-experiences have value for persons of all ages. Learning by doing and having opportunities to practice a new skill under supervision often help persons gain confidence in their ability.

Small group work may provide an opportunity for persons who will not contribute in a large group to become actively involved. Some tasks lend themselves to smaller groups. However, some older persons may want anonymity and small groups may be threatening to them. Having some choice in which group and/or in which task one participates makes small group work less threatening to older persons.

Role-play makes use of pantomime and dialogue as persons spontaneously act out a given situation or relationship in order to develop empathy and insight or to seek a solution to a problem. It enables older adults to consider possible solutions that they might otherwise hesitate to examine. Assuming an assigned role provides freedom.

Simulation games[31] provide a certain social context where structure and relationships are predetermined by the rules. Persons are enabled to experience particular environments and conditions which simulate real-life circumstances and decisions.

Liturgy and *ritual acts* are described by John H. Westerhoff III as ways to "equip and motivate persons and the community to act in the world for social change."[32] They hold potential as appropriate ways of enabling persons to become whole and, as such, may be methodologies for religious education.

This sampling of possible methodologies is not meant to be exhaustive. Several excellent resources which deal with ways of teaching adults are available and give specific help in how to teach.[33]

Facilitating Learning

Laboratory research has been used to develop plans for teaching older adults.[34] It suggests things like using organizational aids, providing feedback, encouraging self-pacing, and eliminating irrelevant stimuli. One can achieve a great deal by remaining cognizant of the abilities and limitations of older adult learners and by using common sense within the context of a dialogical learning environment.

Reuel Howe makes a distinction between dialogue as a principle and as a method. Dialogue as a principle means that persons are open to one another. It requires a willingness to speak honestly, to listen with an open mind to others, and then to respond to what one hears. Many different methods can use the dialogical principle.

Developing environments which encourage dialogue and enabling persons to engage in dialogue can help persons overcome defensiveness so that they become better able to build and sustain relationships. Dialogue can transform the meaning of experiences and can point persons toward new possibilities.[35]

In examining how one can facilitate religious learning, Wayne Rood[36] asserts that the art of teaching as it relates to faith is really "the art of enabling dialogue." He points to Martin Buber's interpretation of dialogue as "a living, mutual relation." Dialogical teaching involves persons who acknowledge individuality as they encounter the content of faith together. It requires creativity. It is never only transmission; rather, it enables discovery on the part of all learners and can be redemptive.

Christian religious education understood as encounter with God must take seriously God's self-disclosure (revelation), the content of the faith, the teacher, and the learner. Religious education takes place within a community of faith and needs to be dialogical on several levels.

The Judeo-Christian traditions affirm that God has already disclosed and is disclosing Godself to all persons in order that they might be in relationship with God, themselves and others. There is also the content which the faith community values and seeks to share through religious education.

Teacher and learner each bring who they are to the teaching-learning experience. They bring their beliefs and their questions, their hurts and their hopes.

Thus, the teaching-learning experience may be facilitated by a teacher who has planned the educational experience. But both teacher and learner have been addressed by God. The teacher has made a positive response to God's self-disclosure, and now he or she both knows and is motivated by the content and lifestyle of the faith. Teachers reach out to the learner on behalf of the faith community in order to engage in dialogue with the learner about God's self-disclosure and the attitudes, beliefs, and lifestyles that uphold the faith community.[37]

What takes place, then, is multidimensional and interactive. It is planned by teacher or, ideally, by teacher and learners. But it is open to and responsive to God's Word, to the faith community's Story and Vision, and to the stories and visions of the learners. It acknowledges that God's Spirit is at work in the teaching-learning encounter and in the world.

One approach to Christian religious education which builds on this dialogical approach and provides an excellent model for facilitating learning has been labeled "shared praxis." Thomas Groome describes shared praxis as "a group of Christians sharing in dialogue their critical reflection on present action in light of the Christian Story and its Vision toward the end of lived Christian faith."[38]

The process, as Groome interprets it, has five components. The process begins with 1) *present action*. Present action might be described as a flash picture of one's self in the world as we portrayed it in Diagram 4.4. It includes one's life history, one's social environment, and all the factors that impinge on one's self-understanding at a given time.

Then 2) *critical reflection* on one's present action is required. If one views the flow of one's life as a river, then it is at this point in the teaching/learning process that one is able to step out of the river and reflect on the course one's life is taking.[39] This enables one to think critically about one's past and to imagine creatively about one's future. Thus, critical reflection enables one to discover and enlarge one's own story.

3) This *dialogue* is with one's self, with others in the faith

community, and with God. It critically reflects on one's present action, allowing persons to experience communication that can become communion. That is to say, as the grace of God becomes operative in relationships, true dialogue can be a means whereby human interaction (communication) is transformed so that persons can become open and vulnerable without fear of rejection (communion). Dialogue allows self-disclosure because "the power to become is both a right and an empowering."[40]

Once persons have acknowledged their present, have reflected critically on it, and have engaged in dialogue about it, they are ready to hear and experience 4) *the Story*. Thomas Groome describes the Christian Story as "the whole faith tradition of our people however that is expressed or embodied."[41] Story includes Scripture and tradition. It includes God's mighty acts in history which can be supremely understood in the life, death, and resurrection of Jesus Christ.

Hearing the Story must not be confused with knowing *about* it. Really hearing or knowing the Story involves one's whole being; it means participating in the Story.[42]

Finally, persons are invited into 5) *the Vision* that arises from the Story. This means that religious education is less than it can be until persons are invited to make a living response to God within the community of faith. Persons are called to respond in faith and love to God's promise in the Story so that they may know who they are and who they can become.

There are five movements in this shared praxis approach to Christian religious education. Thomas Groome describes them as:

1) Naming present action
2) Examining the participants' stories and visions
3) Encountering the faith community's Story and Vision

4) Dialoging between Story and participants' stories

5) Dialoging between Vision and participants' visions.[43]
The fifth movement, then, calls for a response. In light of all one has seen and heard, what is each individual going to do?

This process can facilitate learning for older adults. It can maximize the rich and varied life experiences of older adults and, at the same time, provide them with a concrete beginning point from which to hear and/or rehear the Story and Vision of the faith community.

A shared praxis approach recognizes that older adults bring diverse and sometimes conflicting experiences and beliefs to a teaching-learning experience. It recognizes and affirms those differences and, through a dialogical process, encourages them to recognize and affirm both the common concerns and the unique concerns within the group.

Relating those varied concerns (their stories) to the faith community's Story can (and should) remain dialogical. There is no need for arriving at one answer. Rather, persons are encouraged to understand insights and viewpoints that vary. They can seek meaning(s) that help them make sense of who they are and what life and death mean. Finally, each person is invited to respond in faith—to decide what they will do. Once again, a wide range of responses are possible and ought to be affirmed. In this understanding there is no one, right faith response.

A shared praxis approach is ideal for older adults because it is nonthreatening; it allows persons to name what it is they want to explore; it recognizes and encourages diversity; it begins with persons' life experiences; it enables persons to respond in an open-ended way that encourages persons to continue their pilgrimage of becoming. It addresses the whole person and can lead to reaffirmation and/or change that is believed, felt, willed, and acted upon.

Evaluating Teaching-Learning Experiences

Learning is generally assumed to involve some change in the learner. It can mean intellectual growth involving a reorganization of one's ideas and/or the discovery of new ideas. Change can also involve gaining appreciation for something or someone. Attitudes and feelings can change. Lifestyles can be altered. Persons can develop new skills and abilities.

Learning does not always lead to growth because change is not always positive. It is a mistake to say, "I didn't learn anything at Sunday School today." Persons did "learn" something. It may have been that new persons are not made to feel welcome or that the teacher has an ego problem and won't listen to others' ideas. But persons are affected—changed—in some way by everything they experience.

Our concern is to evaluate planned learning experiences for older adults. It is clear that our evaluation will need to be comprehensive. It will need to consider the context, the content, and the methodology in light of the abilities and needs of the participants.

Evaluation may be defined as a process whose primary purpose is "to find out how much change and growth have taken place as a result of educational experiences."[44] That change and growth can be measured in light of the purposes and objectives of an educational experience.

David Peterson[45] points out that three important factors determine the quality of evaluation. One is the degree of clarity and specificity with which needs have been identified. Another is the extent to which the objectives are clear and measurable. Finally, one needs to determine how the tasks or activities have been completed and how well the issues addressed have been resolved or achieved.

Evaluation is concerned both with the process and with the product or results. David Peterson identifies four steps in the evaluative process: 1) operational objectives must be identified, 2) appropriate methods for measuring objectives must be determined, 3) results need to be compared to an agreed upon standard, and 4) the results need to be shared with interested persons and incorporated in future planning.

Evaluation is a necessary component of the teaching-learning process. Without it, there can be no accountability. Evaluation is a tool and the method of evaluation should be an appropriate means of assessing the learning in order to improve the teaching-learning process. An appropriate evaluation tool takes into account who the learners are and the objectives and methods of the learning; it means that it is valid and relevant.[46]

Not all changes are easily measured. This is especially true for conditions like spiritual well-being.[47]

In addition, we may not always ask the right questions. For example, we might do an extensive evaluation after a lenten Bible study group and completely miss the fact that for several of the participants it was the experience of acceptance and the expressions of love from the group that enabled them to face life. They could begin living again because they were able to resolve the grief which they were experiencing after the death of their spouses.

The easiest things to measure are generally not the most significant. For example, it is easy to count participants and to determine whether or not a program lost money, paid for itself, or made money. Length of time spent can be easily measured also, but that should not be confused with amount of growth.

All changes which occur in a teaching-learning process are not of equal importance. Weighing the importance of what is learned should take into account the basic assumptions and goals of a given community. For instance, the completion of Bible study workbooks may be less significant (though easier to determine) than one's attitudes and behavior towards the young persons in one's community who chose not to register for the draft.

Effective evaluation is an ongoing process. It ought not be used *only* at the completion of an educational experience. Teachers need to be continuously engaged in evaluation. As one prepares to teach, questions like these should be informing one's planning:

Do I understand the needs and goals of my students as they perceive them?

What subject matter would appropriately speak to our objectives?

What resources will aid us in achieving our goal(s)?

What methods will best move us toward our goal(s)?

Can our meeting facilities be changed to improve our ability to teach and learn?

How can I get feedback that will help in planning where and how we go from here?

As one teaches, one needs to remain sensitive to what is working well and what is ineffective. Ongoing evaluation requires one to be willing to adapt one's teaching plan as one goes. It is important to point out, however, that this kind of flexibility is *not* the same thing as "winging it."

It requires more planning, not less. It means being so

familiar with the topic and possible ways of approaching it, that one is free to respond to group needs as they emerge.

Learners need to be integrally involved in this ongoing evaluation process. Their involvement should take a wide variety of appropriate forms. Sometimes a brief oral review of where we are, where we want to go, and how we might get there is helpful. Sometimes a questionnaire will yield valuable information. At other times, letting persons know that their input is always needed and welcome may suffice. Periodic conferences between teacher and learner can serve as an evaluative tool. Using a group planning technique can be, in fact, an effective means of evaluation.

Older learners often exhibit a great deal of anxiety over evaluation. They generally resist evaluation that focuses on the learners and their achievements. Thus, David Peterson proposes that for older adults, evaluation ought to assess how the learners felt about the experience, how relevant it was to their needs, and how effective they thought the teacher was in presenting and clarifying issues. Rediagnosis of the older learners' needs ought to be the primary purpose of evaluation rather than measuring the learners' progress.[48]

Soon after the teaching-learning experience, the teacher needs to sit down and review what happened, making use of whatever learner input one has. What happened? What was the best part of the experience? What was the weakest part? How can it be improved next time? Is progress being made toward the group's goals? Are the goals being altered by the process? If so, is it the intent of the group to buy into the new goals? What are the next steps which will facilitate individual and group progress toward their goals. Only then is the teacher in a position to begin planning for the next teaching-learning experience.

The recognition that goals may be altered unknowingly as the learning process evolves is important. It may be perfectly appropriate for goals to change. But it is important that both teacher and learners recognize and agree on what the goals are or are becoming. This leads us to highlight an important but often neglected component of the evaluative process. Rediagnosing learner needs[49] at regular intervals is important for all persons. It is requisite to lifelong learning.

Conclusion

Teaching older adults must be grounded in an understanding of the resources older learners bring and the demands being made on them as they come to participate in a teaching-learning experience. Persons who choose to teach older adults need to engage in self-assessment in order to better understand the strengths and weaknesses they bring as a teacher of older adults.

Planning a learning experience that engages learners in the process and encourages critical thinking about both the underlying assumptions and the process on the part of all learners is crucial. The planning cycle needs to be an ongoing process that gives attention to underlying assumptions, the needs of individuals and groups, setting goals, selecting resources, creating a growth enhancing learning environment, choosing appropriate methodologies, facilitating the teaching-learning experience, and evaluating in ways that cycle back into goal setting for future teaching-learning experiences.

Teaching older adults in and for a faith community involves more than imparting knowledge. It means participating in a teaching-learning experience in such a way that persons are enabled to grow in faith and love. We will examine how this can be done in chapter six.

Chapter Five Notes

1. Dougles C. Kimmel, *Adulthood and Aging* (New York: John Wiley & Sons, 1974), p. 379.

2. For an excellent summary of this model, see Keith Main, "The Power-Load-Margin Formula of Howard Y. McClusky as the Basis for a Model of Teaching," *Adult Education*, Vol. 30, No. 1 (1979), pp. 19–33. Or see Howard Y. McClusky, "Education for Aging: the Scope of the Field and Perspectives for the Future," in *Learning for Aging* (Washington, D.C.: Adult Education Association, n.d.), pp. 324–355.

3. Howard Y. McClusky, "The Adult as Learner" in *Management of the Urban Crisis*, Stanley E. Seashore and Robert J. McNeill, eds. (New York: The Free Press, 1971), p. 514.

4. For a comprehensive and detailed analysis of needs assessment with adult learners, see K. Patricia Cross, "Adult Learners: Characteristics, Needs, and Interests," in Richard E. Peterson and Associates, eds. *Lifelong Learning in America* (San Francisco: Jossey-Bass, 1979), pp. 75–141.

5. Main, "The Power-Load-Margin Formula of Howard Y. McClusky" p. 21. Reprinted with permission granted by the American Association for Adult and Continuing Education (AAACE).

6. I am indebted to Arthur C. Burman, professor of adult education at the University of Iowa, for his helpful insights on the enabling role of teachers with adults.

7. Thomas Merton, *The Seven Storey Mountain* (New York: Harcourt, Brace, 1948), pp. 139–140.

8. David A. Peterson, *Facilitating Education for Older Learners* (San Francisco: Jossey-Bass, 1983), p. 152.

9. These groups ranged in size from twenty to forty-four and included a graduate class in adult education at the University of Iowa, a group of United Methodist teachers of adults, and forty-four older adult learners who were interviewed by Vogel for her doctoral thesis.

10. Harry Overstreet, *Leaders for Adult Education* (New York: American Association for Adult Education, 1941).

11. J. R. Kidd, *How Adults Learn,* rev. ed. (New York: Association Press, 1973), especially chapter 11; also see Malcolm Knowles, *The Modern Practice of Adult Education* (New York: Association Press, 1970).

12. Mary Elizabeth Moore, *Education for Continuity and Change: A New*

Model for Christian Religious Education (Nashville, Tennessee: Abingdon Press, 1983), p. 70.

13. Kidd, *How Adults Learn*, p. 266.

14. Maurice L. Monette, "Need Assessment: A Critique of Philosophical Assumptions," *Adult Education*, Vol. XXIX, No. 2 (1979), p. 92. An example of this kind of an approach to education can be found in Paulo Friere, *Pedagogy of the Oppressed* (New York: Herder and Herder, 1970).

15. Charles R. Foster, *Teaching in the Community of Faith* (Nashville, Tennessee: Abingdon, 1982), pp. 128–129.

16. Monette, "Needs Assessment," p. 92.

17. These principles are discussed by Victor M. Agruso, Jr. in *Learning in the Later Years: Principles of Educational Gerontology* (New York: Academic Press, 1978). Also see Kimmel, *Adulthood and Aging*, pp. 376–386 and Peterson, *Facilitating Education for Older Learners*, pp. 146–166.

18. Kidd, *How Adults Learn*, p. 46.

19. Robert J. Havighurst, "Education through the Adult Life Span," in *Educational Gerontology*, No. 1 (1976), pp. 41–52. Also see Robert J. Havighurst, *Developmental Tasks and Education*, 3rd ed. (New York: McKay, 1972).

20. Alan B. Knox, *Adult Development and Learning* (San Francisco: Jossey-Bass, 1977), p. 426.

21. Summarized by Monette in "Needs Assessment", p. 85.

22. Ibid., pp. 87–94.

23. Cf. Kidd, *How Adults Learn*, chapter 9; and Roger Heimstra, *Lifelong Learning* (Lincoln, Nebraska: Professional Educators Publications, Inc., 1976), chapter 6.

24. Leon McKenzie, *The Religious Education of Adults* (Birmingham, Alabama: Religious Education Press, 1982), pp. 218–225.

25. U.S. Department of Health, Education and Welfare, Public Health Service, *Health in the Later Years of Life* (Rockville, Maryland: National Center for Health Statistics, October, 1971).

26. Benjamin A. Bloom, ed., *Taxonomy of Educational Objectives: Handbook I, Cognitive Domain* (New York: David McKay, 1956), pp. 201–207.

27. J. P. Guilford, *Intelligence, Creativity and their Educational Implications* (San Diego: Robert R. Knapp, 1968), pp. 81–96.

28. Byron G. Massialas and Jack Zevin, *Creative Encounters in the Classroom: Teaching and Learning Through Discovery* (New York: John Wiley & Sons, 1967), pp. 11–16.

29. See Leonard Steinberg, "Creativity as a Character Trait: An Expanding Concept" in John C. Gowan, George D. Demos, and E. Paul Torrance, *Creativity: Its Educational Implications* (New York: John Wiley & Sons, 1969), pp. 124–137.

30. David R. Krathwohl, Benjamin S. Bloom, and Bertram B. Masia,

Taxonomy of Educational Objectives: Handbook II, Afffective Domain (New York: David McKay, 1964), pp. 176–185.

31. See Dennis Benson, *Gaming* (Nashville, Tennessee: Abingdon Press, 1971) for information on how to create and use simulation games.

32. John H. Westerhoff III, "The Liturgical Imperative of Religious Education," in *The Religious Education We Need: Toward the Renewal of Christian Education,* James Michael Lee, ed. (Birmingham, Alabama: Religious Education Press, 1977), p. 82.

33. A general handbook for teachers of adults is *Adult Education Procedures: A Handbook of Tested Patterns for Effective Participation* by Paul Bergevin, Dwight Morris, and Robert M. Smith (New York: Seabury, 1963). An excellent book which deals with ways of teaching within a Christian context is by Wayne Rood, *The Art of Teaching Christianity* (Nashville, Tennessee, Abingdon Press, 1968). A helpful book focusing on ministry with older persons is Donald F. Clingan, *Aging Persons in the Community of Faith* (Indianapolis, Indiana: Indiana Commission on the Aging and Aged for the Institute on Religion and Aging, 1975). Another excellent resource is Leon McKenzie, *The Religious Education of Adults* (Birmingham, Alabama: Religious Education Press, 1982), chapter 8.

34. For a review of literature on older adults' abilities to learn which suggests ways to improve their performance, see Morris A. Okun, "Implications of Gerepsychological Research for the Instruction of Older Adults" in *Adult Education,* Vol. XXVII, No. 3, (1977), pp. 139–155.

35. See Reuel L. Howe, *The Miracle of Dialogue* (New York: Seabury, 1963). For a detailed analysis of the dialogue theory, see James Michael Lee, *The Flow of Religious Instruction* (Birmingham, Alabama: Religious Education Press, 1973), pp. 180–188. In spite of Lee's critique, I find this to be a helpful model. My own theological assumptions include the belief that God's Spirit is active in the teaching-learning process and that "it is God who teaches, not we. Through us and with us, God continues the work of creation and redemption begun so long ago. And there in that work, as co-teachers, we do indeed meet the last word, the first word, God's Word—Jesus Christ" (*Foundations for Teaching and Learning in the United Methodist Church,* p. 82).

36. Wayne Rood, *The Art of Teaching Christianity* (Nashville, Tennessee: Abingdon Press, 1968), chapter 3.

37. Ibid., chapter 2.

38. Thomas H. Groome, *Christian Religious Education: Sharing Our Story and Vision* (San Francisco: Harper & Row, 1980), chapter 9.

39. James Fowler in *Stages of Faith* (New York: Harper & Row, 1981) uses the analogy of a river to describe the flow of our lives. He maintains that at stage 2 of faith development (mythic-literal faith) persons are not yet able to step out of the stream, stand on the bank, and reflect on the

flow of their life; persons at stage 3 (synthetic-conventional faith) do have this ability.

40. Lewis Sherrill, *The Gift of Power*, pp. 121–123; 191–192.

41. Groome, *Christian Religious Education*, p. 192.

42. William Stringfellow, *A Private and Public Faith* (Grand Rapids, Michigan: Eerdmans, 1962), pp. 17–31.

43. Groome, *Christian Religious Education*, chapter 10.

44. Adult Education Association, *Program Evaluation in Adult Education* (Chicago: AEA, 1952).

45. Peterson, *Facilitating Education for Older Learners*, pp. 281–282.

46. These ideas on evaluation are based on the work of Philip D. Langerman, ed., *You Can Be a Successful Teacher of Adults: NSPCAE'S Authoritative Sourcebook and Information Guide* (Washington, D.C.: National Association for Public Continuing and Adult Education, 1974), pp. 170–171; and on Kidd, *How Adults Learn*, pp. 283–291.

47. An entire book has been written to advocate that spiritual well-being is a vitally important contributor to quality of life for older persons; the case is made that spiritual well-being has generally been overlooked by researchers and practitioners working with older adults. See James A. Thorson and Thomas C. Cook, *Spiritual Well-Being of the Elderly* (Springfield, Illinois: Charles C. Thomas, Publisher, 1977). Note especially "Social Indicators of Spiritual Well-Being" by David O. Moberg, pp. 20–34.

48. Peterson, *Facilitating Education for Older Learners*, p. 161.

49. Malcolm Knowles, *The Adult Learner: A Neglected Species* (Houston: Gulf Publishing Company, 1973), p. 122.

CHAPTER SIX

Developing and Implementing Programs of Religious Education for Older Adults

"Old men need a vision, not only recreation.
Old men need a dream, not only a memory.
It takes three things to attain a sense of significant being
> God
> A Soul
> A Moment
The three are always here.
Just to be is a blessing.
Just to live is holy."

(Abraham J. Heschel)

Older adults need to know and accept themselves. They seek to make sense of and find meaning in their lives. This may lead persons to recognize with Job that
"Wisdom is with the aged,
and understanding in length of days" (Job 12:12).
Maslow's hierarchy of needs[1] makes clear that spiritual needs cannot be addressed until physical needs are met. Spiritual well-being is a topic that was examined at the 1971 White House Conference on Aging.[2] At that conference,

"spiritual" was interpreted to include "the source of life, enabling and sustaining values in society, providing the philosophical orientation to all of life, and touching every aspect of human conduct."[3]

Given so broad a definition, spiritual might be "religious, antireligious, or nonreligious."[4] For our purposes, we will focus on spiritual well-being as it can be nurtured and enabled through religious education.

We have affirmed that wholeness is that which persons desire and need; we have suggested that a holistic understanding of persons requires giving heed to their physical, psychological, and social circumstances. In addition, we have shown how persons' basic values and presuppositions affect the way they view the world and their decision-making processes.

Whenever programs are developed, it is crucial that those who engage in planning know and are involved with the intended participants. At the same time, the planners must be honest about who they are, what assumptions they are making, what they hope to accomplish, and why.

Those engaged in planning for religious education are influenced by basic theological, psychological, and educational frameworks. For example, when I plan Christian religious education programs for older adults, I am operating on these premises:

1) Persons are who they are because of their life history, their physical and psychological abilities and deficiencies, their social environment, and their ability to cope with the milestones and/or crises they have experienced as they move through the phases of life.

2) God loves all persons, unconditionally.

3) All persons are offered God's gracious gift of new life in Jesus Christ.

4) Persons are capable of becoming—growing toward wholeness which can be enabled by saying "yes" to God's gift.

5) Being whole means being in right-relationship with self, others, and God.

6) Older adults face the task of resolving the issue of integrity vs. despair as they seek to make sense of death and life.

7) Older adults are capable of growing and learning.

8) Older persons bring rich resources to the teaching-learning experience.

9) Programing for older adults is a task to be done mutually by planners, teachers, and learners.

10) Older adults have a wide variety of needs and, therefore, require a multifaceted educational program.

It is very important for program planners to be clear about the assumptions they make in order to see if these assumptions mesh with the needs and expectations of potential participants.

A Case Study: The Shepherd's Center[5]

In 1972 a small group of church leaders came together because they believed there was a need for a church-related retirement home in Kansas City. They were convinced that the needs of older persons could best be met by a comprehensive, intentional ministry.

They set out to confirm this need, and so they hired a consulting firm to do a feasibility study. The results were somewhat disconcerting. Since only 5 percent of all persons sixty-five and over at any given time live in an institutional setting, the other 95 percent live in communities which are served by churches and synagogues. The issue became one of seeking, intentionally, to meet the needs of older adults who live independently in their houses and apartments.

That small group of church leaders chose the name, "The Shepherd's Center," because it reflects the kind of caring support found in Psalm 23. Basic decisions were made. In order to meet multiple needs, this would need to be an ecumenical effort. The Shepherd's Center would not be a place or a program. Rather, it would be a process that grows out of the needs of persons in a specific population base; it would seek to work with those persons to enable them to remain independent as long as feasible and to find meaning and purpose in their later years.

The stated purposes of The Shepherd's Center became:

1) To sustain older people who desire to live independently in their own homes and apartments in the community;

2) To provide retired people with an opportunity to use their experience, training, and skills in significant social roles;

3) To enhance life satisfaction in later maturity and enable self-realization through artistic expression, community service, caring relationships, lifelong learning, and the discovery of inner resources;

4) To demonstrate life at its best in later maturity so as to provide attractive role models for successful aging;

5) To advocate the right of older people to a fair share of society's goods, and to assist them in gaining access to services;

6) To contribute to knowledge about what is required for successful aging and to experiment with new approaches and programs for meeting the needs of older people.[6]

The Shepherd's Center adopted territorial boundaries—a fifteen square mile area bounded by four specific streets. The area had a population of 53,000, over one-fifth of whom were sixty-five and over. To be eligible for its services, persons had to live in the area and need the service they requested. The volunteers who provide the services function as a check on whether persons qualify, thus eliminating the need for extensive case records.

Services and programs were carefully planned as needs were demonstrated. They were initiated one at a time and on a small scale.

The theological assumption which provides the foundation for The Shepherd's Center is that the Judeo-Christian traditions can be the source for finding meaning and purpose in life. Faith communities are called to nurture and sustain persons because of their views about God and persons.[7]

Needs were assessed by going to where older persons were and asking: "What is it that you need in your life that, if you don't have, life is going to fall apart? What do you have to have in order to survive? Where are you hurting? Where do you have needs so great that unless that particular need is met, life is not going to come together for you?"

It soon became apparent that needs existed at four levels—reflecting Abraham Maslow's insights. These four areas can be used to design an intentional ministry with older adults. "Intentional" implies that ministry is not left to chance. "With" is crucial because "ministry *for* older adults" is bound to fail. Older adults are capable and can be enablers, as well as being enabled, in ministry.

The first area of need has to do with *life maintenance*. Basic human needs like hunger and shelter must be met. Some of these services The Shepherd's Center could meet directly. In other cases, the center could serve as a conduit—linking persons in need with community services that were already available. Duplicating existing services was carefully avoided.

Life maintenance services that have been initiated include Meals-on-Wheels, Handyman, Companion Aids, Shoppers, Wheels that Care, Security and Protection, and Hospice. Care is taken to help those who need help for as long as they need help; care is also taken to see that persons don't sell their independence by remaining dependent longer than necessary.

The second area is *life enrichment*. This aspect of ministry includes adult education which provides coping and life-enriching skills. The Shepherd's Center designed an education program which is called, "Adventures in Learning."

Over 1,400 persons participate in "Adventures in Learning" each year. One day each week for approximately ten weeks, a wide range of courses are offered. A small enrollment fee ($5) entitles persons to participate in as many classes as they wish.

Classes are taught by volunteers—most of whom are themselves older adults. A sampling of classes offered in a recent winter term includes Health Assistance (coordinated by an R.N.), Needlework, Spanish, Home Maintenance, Bible Therapy, Creative Writers Workshop, Travelogue, Book Reviews, Yoga, Wood Carving, The Remembered Past: 1914–1945, International Relations and American Affairs, Music, Macrame, French, What You Should Know About Social Security and Medicare, Nutrition (coordinated by a registered dietician), Basic Drawing, Beginners Bridge, Square Dancing, and Employment Service.

Defensive driving classes and preretirement seminars focus on important areas of concern for older adults. A

Health Enrichment Center focuses on wellness. Creative workships meet on a different day to provide persons with instruction and opportunity to express themselves through arts and crafts. These range from painting and chair caning to quilting and photography to conversational French and building self-esteem.

The third area for intentional ministry is *life reconstruction*. Losses that occur necessitate older adults having to reconstruct their world and their lives. The programs which respond to needs in this area include alcoholism, marriage enrichment, and peer support groups dealing with grief and widowhood.

Some older persons with less well-defined needs benefit from a weekly support group where they can talk and listen to others talk about their lives and concerns. A clinical psychologist who is a devout Roman Catholic is skilled in facilitating a total group of forty or fifty persons in small groups so that they can reexamine and reorganize their lives in a nonthreatening environment. The Shepherd's Center ministers to over 200 persons in this way each year.

The fourth area of intentional ministry is called *life-transcendence*. Its purpose is "to discover the great dimension of mystery and beauty in existence." Judeo-Christian faith communities are called to share their message of "love, justice and mercy—of joy, hope, and life affirmation."[8]

Twenty-five churches and synagogues in the geographical area being served are involved in the support and operation of The Shepherd's Center. They each seek, in their own ways, to supplement this area of ministry through worship, education, and fellowship. Inspirational speakers are scheduled at a noon luncheon on Fridays when "Adventures in Learning" meets.

There is a night team of clergypersons that responds to

calls through a twenty-four-hour answering service. Perhaps most significant of all, the total intentional ministry that is being lived out communicates the love and care of God for all persons.

Implementation requires a large group of committed volunteers. They are enabled by a small, professional staff who serve as program coordinators. The staff works under the direction of a self-perpetuating board of directors who are drawn from participating churches and synagogues as well as the larger community. Effective ministry is dependent on staying in touch with the older persons who are serving and being served. Use is made of community organization skills. Efforts are constantly being made to work in cooperation with public agencies, private business and industry, and unions.

Evaluation is an ongoing process. It focuses more on rediagnosing learners' needs than on measuring what and how much was learned. In addition, participants were asked to judge how effective were individual facilitators.

While this is contrary to a strict operational approach to evaluation, which examines specific behavioral objectives and acceptable levels of performance, it is in keeping with the premise that older adults are able to assess their needs. They are able to decide if their needs are being met, or how they might be better met. There is certainly truth in the statement that older adult learners "evaluate with their feet." They can be expected to come if it meets their needs and to assume responsibility for improving learning opportunities if encouraged to do so. They are apt to stay away if their needs are not met.

At the same time, they can be enabled to engage in double-loop learning which encourages a reexamination of basic values and assumptions as well as of their personal needs. This may lead to a restructuring of their social context as well as to a rediagnosis of their personal needs. This may lead to a restructuring of their own needs.

The work of the center has expanded to provide resources for new centers being established across the country through a Shepherd's Center Network Newsletter and through consulting services.

Developing Programs

A helpful resource for developing intentional ministry with older adults is *Aging Persons in the Community of Faith* by Donald F. Clingan. In it, he depicts a planning cycle (Diagram 6.1) for ministry with older adults which must involve older adults.

Diagram 6.1
The Planning Cycle[9]

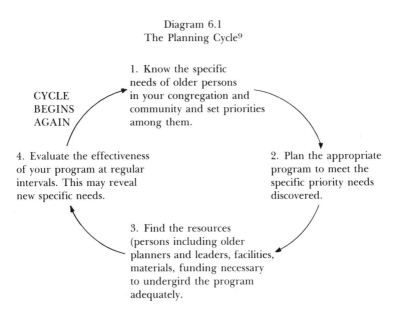

CYCLE BEGINS AGAIN

1. Know the specific needs of older persons in your congregation and community and set priorities among them.

2. Plan the appropriate program to meet the specific priority needs discovered.

4. Evaluate the effectiveness of your program at regular intervals. This may reveal new specific needs.

3. Find the resources (persons including older planners and leaders, facilities, materials, funding necessary to undergird the program adequately.

Program planning should be in response to perceived needs. When it becomes obvious that a need exists, the planning process can commence.

How can we recognize needs? Perhaps the best way is to keep our eyes and ears open. For example, when several newly retired persons are overheard to say that they are bored, it points to a possible need. When food stamp programs are cut, the possibility of having older persons without enough to eat seems likely. When a widow expresses a sense of great loss and fear for her future, there is the possibility that she and others like her have a need that might be addressed.

Using a needs assessment survey[10] is a more formal and systematic way of determining needs for program planning. It can be a helpful tool, but it does not replace developing a sensitivity to what persons are doing and saying. Nor should it rule out the need to reexamine assumptions that planners make.

Once one has an indication that a need exists, it is possible to seek to confirm or refute that assumption. Then if the need is real, it must be clearly stated.

Possible ways of addressing a clearly stated need should be explored. It is good to examine as many alternatives as possible. Representatives from the potential audience should be consulted so that they can provide input. Programs for older adults must provide a number of options since persons' needs are different.

Only then is it time to develop a tentative program, including teaching-learning plans. Developing a plan involves stating one's objectives, deciding on appropriate methodologies for achieving the objectives, and determining the most appropriate setting and the best times for teaching-learning opportunities. Comprehensive programs for ministry with older adults will include many things, as our case study illustrated. We will focus primarily on religious education as one component of that ministry.

Planning must also include ways to promote the planned experiences. The best-laid plans will fail if they are not clearly communicated in an interesting and inviting way to those one hopes to reach.

Errors in determining what the needs are or in assessing how persons might want to address their needs can block the implementation of any religious education program. For example, if program planners determined that widows and widowers in their church needed a support group (which was verified) and in response organized an older singles group (which was perceived as a matchmaking attempt), the plan would be apt to fail. A real need was perceived; the method chosen to meet the need was seen as inappropriate by those they had hoped to reach.

However, it is possible to accurately assess a need and to select an appropriate methodology and still fail. Inappropriate settings and/or poor timing can also block participation. For instance, holding a class at night in winter may keep persons away who would otherwise participate. Many older women who live alone do not go out after dark. They may not drive at night; they may be afraid of falling; they may fear being vulnerable to crime. Holding a class in a large room with poor acoustics and background noise from a day-care center, may cause interested persons to stay away because they fear they could not hear.

Once the first meeting time arrives, those who respond should be given an opportunity to get acquainted and then to examine the tentative teaching-learning plan in order to make suggestions and alterations.

It is quite possible and appropriate for a facilitator/teacher to guide a group in making major changes in the tentative teaching-learning plan. A word of warning is necessary here. It is *not* appropriate, in my judgment, to decide that since the teaching-learning plan is tentative anyway, it will be better to just have a general plan and then ask the group what they want to do. On the other hand, it is detrimental for planners to feel that they have made so much investment in making a plan that alterations are perceived as personal affronts.

One danger is that planners will consider what is convenient for themselves rather than what will be most convenient for the prospective audience. I made this error recently when (as it turned out) I correctly assessed the need of pastors and persons working in adult education in local churches who were seeking new insight and understanding about faith development. I selected a lecture/seminar approach (which was finally evaluated positively) and scheduled it for four Saturday mornings (a convenient time for a college teacher with many responsibilities during the week). When the first day came, four highly motivated persons attended—two of whom would have to miss one or more of the scheduled sessions. We looked at my tentative teaching-learning plan and I asked for suggestions to make it fit their needs. In the course of the discussion, it became clear that others were really interested in the topic, but prior time commitments and/or the travel time and distance involved had blocked their participation. The group determined that an all-day eight hour seminar on a Tuesday, would be more appropriate than four two-hour sessions on Saturday. It would be scheduled two months later to allow for adequate time for promotion.

When the scheduled Tuesday arrived, thirteen interested participants ventured out in a snowstorm. Better timing was the key to success.

The group's major alteration to my plan did not make it perfect. As a teacher, I would not choose to introduce persons to a topic like faith development in one large block of time. Even so, I learned that, in this case, timing was more of a determinant for participation than the need to deal with smaller amounts of material and to allow time for internalizing new concepts.

By the end of the first meeting or class, the teaching-learning plan should be "owned" by the group. Every participant should realize that owners have the right-even the responsibility—to improve what they own. Responsibility for implementing the teaching-learning plan now rests with the group—teachers and learners alike.

As we have seen, evaluation is an integral part of the planning process. It needs to be viewed by both teachers and learners as a group responsibility.

The primary purpose of evaluation is to rediagnose needs and to strengthen the teaching-learning process as it is being experienced. That means that it should not be left until the end; rather, evaluation is an interactive, ongoing process. It should include examining the goals for the specific teaching-learning experience as well as the goals for the comprehensive religious education program.

To summarize, developing a religious education program with older adults should include the following steps:

1) Recognize possible need(s)
2) Contact representative persons from potential audiences to
   a. Seek to confirm need(s)
   b. Clarify what the need(s) is (are)

    c. Explore a wide variety of options
    d. Examine critically the underlying values and assumptions which undergird the development of teaching-learning plans for addressing need(s)
3. Develop a tentative program
    a. Objectives
    b. Methods
    c. Settings
    d. Timing
4) Promote program including specific teaching-learning opportunities
5) Present tentative teaching-learning plan to persons who respond
6) Implement plan with alterations as appropriate
7) Evaluate teaching-learning experience and its underlying assumptions
8) Evaluate teaching-learning experience in light of total program objectives

Programing and Government Programs

One way the church can engage in ministry with older persons is to work for the passage of federal, state, and local legislation that will be beneficial to older persons. It is time that religious institutions recognize that they are called to work for social justice. One way to do that is to study the political issues of the day and to work within the system to bring about constructive changes that affirm the worth and dignity of all persons.[11]

Aging has been the concern of politicians for a number of years. That concern manifested itself in the Older American Act of 1965 as ammended. An extensive network of federal, state, and area agencies was created to deal with the needs of aging persons. Now, however, budget cuts, and the threat of even greater cutbacks, suggest that there may be less support for programs that benefit the elderly.

It seems necessary for religious groups to find ways to support and supplement existing government programs. Elbert Cole[12] has suggested that persons of faith might do well to support national governmental support for providing 1) health care and long-term health maintenance and 2) income maintenance for the old. Then communities of faith and other local agencies might assume responsibility for other social programs that have been funded in the past by Titles III, V, and VII of the Older Americans Act. These include multipurpose senior centers, nutrition programs including congregate meal sites and home delivered meals (III); training and recruiting of persons in the field of aging, multidisciplinary gerontology centers (IV); and community based employment services and programs (V).

The key seems to be to work for legislation that seems to be in the best interests of the elderly and society as a whole, to supplement and work cooperatively with government programs that exist[13], to avoid duplicating existing services, and to develop programs where needs that are not being met are found to exist.

Volunteers and Programing

Much of the work of religious institutions is carried on by volunteers. This practice is undergirded by a theology of the ministry of the laity (*laos:* people of God). Indeed, discipleship may be understood in terms of being a witness for and serving God in every area of one's life.

Wesner Fallaw[14] and others have made the case that volunteerism is no substitute for professionally trained pastor-teachers. There have certainly been problems revolving around what expectations can be made, how quality control and standards are to be maintained, and what knowledge and skills volunteer teachers in the church bring to the teaching-learning process.

Nevertheless, both protestant and Roman Catholic churches have relied heavily on volunteer teachers for Sunday Schools, CCD classes, Vacation Bible Schools, and a wide variety of study groups. It is my contention that ministry with older adults provides a real opportunity for volunteers. Many older adults have valuable experience, knowledge, and skills for becoming trained volunteers engaged in teaching-learning opportunities in their church or synagogue. Older adults may have both more time and more experience to share than any other group of persons within a faith community.

A book written for laity and clergy maintains that to be the church requires that all Christians—children, young people, and adults of all ages—must respond to the call to be sent out into the world "with the liberating, saving, ministering power of the Gospel of Jesus Christ."[15]

Laity tend to see their call to serve either within the church or in the world on behalf of the church.[16] They are, in fact, called to serve God both within and beyond their faith community. The ministry of faith communities is lived out through the lives of their members.

In the last decade, much has been written on volunteerism. It has become increasingly clear that there is much power available when volunteers are trained well, placed appropriately, and nourished meaningfully.[17]

Faith communities, in a way that is unique among institutions dependent on volunteers, seek to nurture and educate their members so that they will identify with and own the ministry of their faith community.[18] Volunteering (i.e., serving) can be an end as well as a means to an end. Some persons find fulfillment from serving others, apart from the positive benefits which result from their voluntary efforts.

Peter Berger and Thomas Luckmann[19] provide insights about the social construction of reality. In their view, legitimizing rationale can grow out of a faith community's value structure and orientation. James Wood[20] builds on this concept when he asserts that value-fostering organizations, such as religious institutions, may stand on biblically based concepts like justice and compassion. This enables them to claim legitimacy for positions and actions which may be more liberal than the specific views held by many of their members. Wood claims it is possible to raise the rank of such values, in terms of members' value hierarchies, when fundamental, general religious values are brought to bear on specific issues.[21]

A faith community which decides to be intentional about a comprehensive ministry with older adults can develop a program for training, placing, and nurturing volunteers which is rooted in biblical and theological understandings; through it they can accomplish a wide variety of objectives. Clingan maintains that it is feasible to accomplish "1) the reshaping of social attitudes toward age and the aging, 2) the redirecting of social trends involving the elderly, 3) the spiritual preparation of all ages for old age, and 4) the permeation of the whole of congregation and community with reverence for the old and the aging process of life."

In the process, the faith community can be enabled to "1) become an instigator of a system of values for individuals and society which upholds the significance of the aged and 2) act in compassion and understanding toward the aged, protecting them when they need protection, enabling them to give creatively of themselves and helping them to achieve their rights as human beings."[22]

The community which the volunteer serves is not the only one to benefit from the involvement. A study made by the Ethel Percey Andrus Gerontology Center[23] indicates that there are many benefits which accrue to the older volunteer as well. These include a broader and more realistic assessment of life, participation in a worthwhile activity in the context of a warm and accepting environment which results in better emotional health, opportunities for intergenerational contacts which foster mutual respect, and intellectual growth which develops problem-solving skills and abilities.

There are mutual benefits for both older volunteers and the faith community which can grow out of a well-conceived and constantly nurturing program. This kind of program enables older volunteers to engage in ministry with and for their faith community.

Making Use of Existing Programs

Old-age education is needed for persons of all ages. Its purposes are twofold: 1) to prepare persons to accept and deal creatively with their own aging, and 2) to help persons understand and deal responsibly and compassionately with the old.[24]

A program for comprehensive ministry will generally include both facets. It will make use of existing programs and groups and will seek to sensitize and provide resources so that they can assume responsibility for old-age education.

For example, church-school classes are ready-made vehicles for achieving this purpose. The kindergarten class might engage in education on aging as a part of their Thanksgiving unit. They might visit the apple orchard of a retired farmer and watch him make apple cider. Learning new skills from experienced older persons is something for which to be thankful. Then they might take cider to a nursing home and share it with the residents there. They can learn that one way of giving thanks is to serve others.

The fifth-grade class might adopt-a-grandparent as a project during their unit on discipleship. The junior-high class might offer their services for a day to older persons in the church or community when they are studying self-giving love.

The high-school class might study growing old at a weekend retreat. Aging simulations[25] and a number of movies[26] provide excellent beginning points. One of the most effective ways to sensitize young people to the sensory losses and physical limitations which aging may bring is to simulate those losses.

Have students wear a pair of work gloves (arthritis), put dampened cotton balls in their ears (hearing loss), and put two thicknesses of saran wrap over their eyes (glaucoma). Simulate stiff joints in some students by using an elastic bandage to secure a folded up newspaper behind their knees. Then proceed to deal with the topic of aging. Show a film and discuss it. Take a break and ask the students to make a telephone call, buy decaffeinated pop or coffee from a coin operated machine (they may not take off their gloves) and go to the bathroom. After the break, continue the simulation by having them write down their feelings.

At this point end the simulation and spend time debriefing. I have found that real empathy emerges. The energy required to do simple tasks, the frustration resulting from having trouble seeing and hearing, the extra time and caution required to find coins and dial the telephone, and the tendency to withdraw always surface in discussions I have led.

It is important to emphasize that not all older persons experience all of these problems. Even so, there are good reasons why older people drive slower or stand in the middle of the aisle when they first enter a church before proceeding to their pew. Increased understanding results.

A class for middle-aged persons might focus on coping with aging parents[27]. The older adult class might study books like Paul Tournier's, *Learn to Grow Old* or Reuel Howe's *How to Stay Young While Growing Older*.

These examples are only meant to jog your mind regarding the myriad opportunities for education on aging that could enrich existing classes and units of study. Programing need *not* mean creating new programs and groups. Rather, the first task of a program coordinator is to make use of existing programs and groups.

When needs exist and no existing program or group can be equipped to meet those needs, programs should be planned carefully and then begun on a small scale. One way to enhance the effectiveness of coordinators is to give them complete responsibility for recruiting and enabling volunteers, for refining and improving the program, and for working directly with the program so that they receive feedback from both the volunteers and the program participants.

Coordinators may be accountable to an advisory board, a council on ministry, or a staff person. They should understand to whom they are responsible and should receive support and feedback from that person or group on a regular basis.

In programs involving ministry with older adults, coordinators are most often volunteers. When possible, it is good to recruit older adults to serve as coordinators for these programs. We have already seen how this is being effectively done by The Shepherd's Center.[28]

Coordinators need organizational skills and skills in working with people. They need to understand why a particular program exists and be flexible enough to see it grow and change. They need to be willing to let it die if and when its task is done.

Implementing Programs

Religious education programs often depend heavily on volunteers, as we have seen. Persons are willing to do things when they see a need and believe their action can help.

Churches and synagogues do many things unwittingly which communicate a lack of sensitivity and care for older persons.[29] For example, a congregation might begin by looking at their facilities from the point of view of persons who have difficulty with steps or are confined to a wheelchair. They might look at their program from the point of view of persons who do not go out at night. They might do an inventory to assess the involvement of older persons.

The four program components adopted by The Shepherd's Center can assist faith communities in maintaining a balanced program that promotes wholeness. We will examine examples of program implementation in each of the four areas: life maintenance, life enrichment, life reconstruction, and life transcendence.

It is important to point out that religious institutions neither can nor should try to be all things to all people.

Churches and synagogues must care about the whole person and be responsive to their needs. But this does not mean that religious institutions must meet all needs. Rather, they can work with other agencies, be aware of and refer persons to governmental and private agencies which provide needed services, and lobby for legislation which will be just and responsive to persons in need. When needs exist that cannot be met through other agencies or in other ways, then religious institutions and/or persons of faith must find appropriate ways to address and meet those needs.

Life Maintenance

An obvious contribution religious groups make to a ministry for the elderly is by founding and maintaining retirement homes. This is a significant ministry and will, no doubt, continue in spite of serious legal and financial problems which are calling religious bodies to greater accountability.[30]

But what of 95 percent of the population of persons sixty-five and over who do not need institutionalization? How can religious institutions enable them to remain independent? What services address the needs older adults have that will assist them in maintaining their independence?

Programs in the following areas have been identified by Clingan.[31]

1) Consumer Issues

Programs in consumer education can be especially helpful. In addition to helping older adults find ways to get more for their dollar, these programs can address consumer fraud. Old persons are often victimized in this way.

A cooperative buying program is another way to assist older adults. Many churches and synagogues engage in or provide facilities for food cooperatives. This is a form of ministry that is not limited only to older adults, though they can benefit from it if attention is given to solving any transportation problems they may have.

2) Health

Many older persons avoid going to a doctor if at all possible. Providing health screening services for conditions such as blood pressure, diabetes, anemia, and glaucoma can serve an important function. These services can be effectively done by volunteer nurses in conjunction with churchwide events like a fall festival where participation of older members is desired. If other community agencies are already providing health screening services, the church or synagogue might organize transportation to the screening site.

Making persons aware of home health services (public health nursing or hospice) and mail order drug services (like that available through AARP) can aid persons in solving problems that appeared insurmountable. Health education classes which focus on wellness and wholeness can recognize the interrelatedness between physical, mental, and spiritual well-being. The faith community is in an enviable position both to reach older persons and to foster a holistic approach to wellness.

3) Housing

One of the potentially traumatic decisions older adults may face is whether they will be able, physically and/or financially, to remain in their home. Sometimes leaving one's too-large home necessitates leaving one's friends and neighborhood and faith community. If they decide to move, they are faced with deciding whether to go into an apartment or a retirement center, or to move in with a child, a sibling, or a friend. Peer-support groups that allow persons to talk about their fears and to examine alternatives before a decision must be made, can be extremely valuable.

Providing a "handyman" file, so that persons who want odd jobs and persons who require minor home repairs can help one another, is a relatively simple task to organize and implement.

4) Legal Services

Some churches and synagogues provide legal aid to older persons. If there are other groups performing such services, the faith community might assume responsibility for making information about such services available to older persons in the community. Advocacy is another function faith communities can serve to bring about justice and insure human dignity for all persons.

Sometimes persons need legal advice regarding conservatorships and guardianships for their aging parents or other relatives. Tax counseling and other financial counseling can help persons protect themselves from making unwise decisions and bequests. Care must be taken that the agency or religious organization providing the counseling avoid doing anything that could be perceived as self-serving.

5) Nutrition

Providing congregate meal sites is a service many faith communities engage in. Interpreting that program to others is another vital service persons of faith can perform. It is sad to hear persons complain that "Mr. B. has a million dollars in the bank and he's always down at the church eating for a dollar a day!" Persons who say things like that fail to realize that good nutrition (which Mr. B. could afford) is only one goal of congregate meal programs. Having fellowship and socializing with others is a need that persons have regardless of their bank balance.

Nutrition education, including understanding how medications and diets interact, is important. This need can be met by groups which meet to share in a pot-luck meal (many widows miss having an excuse to make a favorite recipe) and then have speakers who address topics of interest.

Many religious groups participate in and/or coordinate home-delivered meals. This program not only enables house-bound persons to remain in their own homes, but it also provides purpose and meaning for persons who deliver the meals.

6) Social Support Services

There are a wide range of services which can enable older adults to maintain their independence. This goal is in keeping with a faith community's commitment to enabling wholeness and helping all persons become all that they can be. Examples include shopping services where persons who do not drive are taken to the supermarket where they can buy groceries economically. Telephone reassurance programs communicate care and bring a sense of security to family and friends as well as to those who receive a call everyday. This is a task that some housebound persons can engage in. Thus, they perform a needed ministry and feel better about themselves.

Equipment banks where persons can borrow crutches, wheelchairs, hospital beds, etc., help persons avoid unnecessary expenses at a time when they are already burdened with health and medical bills. It is even possible to just make a file of things persons are willing to loan (from cribs for visiting grandchildren to hospital beds) and then to serve as a broker by putting a loanee in touch with a loaner.

Chore services can work much like the handyman service. Persons who are willing to do light housekeeping or other tasks as they specify can be put in touch with persons who need those services.

One area of great need that is not available in many communities is adult day-care centers.[32] This is a form of ministry that churches and synagogues may be well-equipped to perform because they have facilities which may be available during the week.

Adult education classes can contribute to self maintenance in many ways. In addition to enabling persons to develop maintenance skills, it can bolster one's wavering self-esteem. A seventy-one-year-old man, interviewed by me in my study,[33] said his most important role was "hanging on." This self-understanding was reflected when he said his reason for taking a woodworking class was to prove to himself that he could do it.

Life Enrichment

It is the task of adult educators in general, and religious educators in particular, to provide opportunities to enable older adults to cope and to thrive in a world that is constantly changing. We live in a world where many of the roles attributed to older persons (e.g., retiree, grandparent, nursing home resident) are poorly defined, low-status roles.

As we have seen, older persons face the task of achieving integrity—of making sense of one's life and of affirming the person one has become. Religious education can be a powerful avenue to enable persons to engage in that task.

David Moberg[34] has identified "personal dignity" as one of the spiritual needs of older adults. Religious education can address the need for personal dignity in many different ways.

1) The Old in Ministry

Persons need to be needed. Older persons whose families are grown and who may have retired have time to invest in meaningful ways. Faith communities can equip older persons for ministry so that their self-esteem is affirmed and others benefit from their serving.

Almost everyone can engage in ministry. This was made evident to me when our pastor called on a close friend whose left side was paralyzed by a stroke. The friend was depressed and felt helpless and frustrated. The pastor knew of a *real need* in our faith community and our friend had the ability to meet that need. Several parents had expressed concern about lifestyle choices their teenagers were making. Would our friend pray everyday for these three young persons (whom he knows)? He agreed and later he told me, "You know, I can't walk but I have time and I have my mind and I'm praying for them."

The key is to have real needs—persons recognize busywork at seventy as well as they did at seventeen! Then persons responsible for meeting those needs must provide reinforcement and receive feedback from those engaged in ministry.

Some housebound persons can serve on telephoning committees; some can write personal notes to persons who haven't been participating in the life of the community.

Many older persons are quite capable and mobile. They

may be able to teach, serve in ministries of outreach and evangelism through visitation, work to improve and maintain church facilities, and serve on various church boards and agencies.[35]

It has been said that the 22 million persons who are sixty-five and over in the United States are our greatest natural resource. Certainly, older persons in faith communities bring rich experiences and wisdom that can enrich those communities of which they are a part.

2) Creative Leisure Activities

Older persons who have been socialized into a work-ethic are apt to have trouble knowing how to deal with leisure. Helping persons find ways to use leisure time in order to expand their world and develop their abilities can be fulfilling and lead to increased self-esteem.

Older persons may resist engaging in learning activities, due in part at least to a probable concept of themselves as nonlearners and to an atrophied sense of discovery.[36] These attitudes can and should be overcome through the development of adult education programs that are responsive to the potential participants and their needs.

Arts and crafts classes tend to be popular. One sixty-year-old woman in my study who was enrolled in a woodworking class said she wanted to know how to make things she needed around the house. Her participation in any class was especially significant because her attitude toward formal education was clouded by bitterness because her father had always pushed her to achieve more and do better.

Other persons whom I interviewed indicated that they enrolled in arts and crafts classes for a variety of reasons. One woman enrolled "for my husband," even though she did not tell him that was her real reason. She felt he would need a hobby to help him adjust to his impending retirement so she suggested they enroll in a woodworking class together. A seventy-year-old retired farmer said, "Anyone who has worked all of his life fears retirement." He wanted "something to do." A seventy-four-year-old woman with an eighth-grade education was taking a sewing class because "it's a skill to fall back on." Some were searching for something constructive and enjoyable to occupy their time.

The work ethic was very much in evidence in many of the reasons these older adults gave for participating in adult education. As one person observed, "The harder you study, the better it is!"

3) Self-improvement Classes

Reading groups and book studies, current affairs, signing for the deaf, and applying Scripture to life are examples of self-improvement classes reported on by persons I interviewed. This is an area which both churches and schools can address.

One older woman, a wife and mother of nine, clearly rejected the traditional family roles as central to her self-image. While she acknowledged that her family was important to her, she said she did not think of herself in those terms. What was important to her, was "to enjoy life to the utmost" and to do what she could for others. This self-understanding was reflected in the reasons she gave for participating in adult education classes—"to learn" and "to improve."

Another older woman recognized that she was "in a transition; up in the air; in limbo." Her reasons for participating in a class reflected a desire to escape from boredom and to find meaning in her life.

Persons I interviewed often claimed that the thing they

liked best about adult education classes was a sense of learning and accomplishment. Open discussion, reflecting an environment where they could hear and be heard, and fellowship with other persons were also highly valued.

Six of the twenty-two participants in school-sponsored classes indicated that the class provided an escape from boredom, their normal routine, or their personal problems. One woman seemed to find her painting class provided her with a healthy and constructive outlet after a daily routine of spending hours at the nursing home where she visited her husband and gave him therapy.

Life Reconstruction

Losses characterize old age more than any other life phase. There are predictable changes caused when the last child leaves home and when one retires. There are losses that come when one's health fails or when one is forced to relocate for financial or physical reasons. Death of one's spouse or one's own impending death also cause persons to engage in life reconstruction.

These losses can lead persons to struggle in creative ways so that they grow in wisdom and develop a sense of spiritual well-being. The National Interfaith Coalition on Aging (NICA) has asserted that the spiritual "permeates and gives meaning to all life." It is saying "yes" to life "in spite of negative circumstances." It is acknowledging one's destiny and celebrating one's life as "one grows to accept the past, to be aware and alive in the present, and to live in hope of fulfillment" within the context of a faith community.[37]

Life reconstruction can be enabled by mental health centers and other service providers. However, faith communities seem optimally equipped to engage in a ministry of life reconstruction. As Maggie Kuhn has pointed out:

"Christian nurture . . . ought to deal in a very substantive way with attitudinal change so that people in their middle and later years understand themselves and have built into their own self-images a sturdy approach to the kind of de-meaning, diminishing attitude that society takes toward the human aging process."[38]

Rites of passage are important in every culture and many of them have been acknowledged and celebrated by one's community of faith. For example, birth may be celebrated through baptism; one's marriage and death are lifted up by the faith community. It is important for the faith communi-ty to find appropriate and meaningful ways of dealing with other crises and passages that require persons to recon-struct their lives.

1) Retirement

There are several rites of passage, however, which have traditionally been neglected by both the culture and the faith community. One is retirement. As Maggie Kuhn points out, "Following the 'gold watch' ceremony, there is a great trauma . . . . There is anxiety and fear and a very great loss of self-esteem."[39] Preparation for retirement and celebration of retirement can be sacramental in nature. In it, the faith community can affirm the retiree and can cele-brate "the testimony of a life of faith."[40]

A number of congregations are engaged in preretire-ment education. These programs emphasize 1) "the third age" as a time when persons may experience leisure and give of themselves in service to others and 2) the need to plan for one's future physically, mentally, emotionally, and spiritually. This includes dealing with issues like finances, where one will live, how one will use one's time, and what will give meaning and purpose to life.[41]

This is one example of preventative reconstruction. We

have already seen examples of how classes taken for life enrichment are perceived by some as preparing them to cope with retirement. It should be possible to prepare persons for reconstructing their lives before they fall apart.

2) Death

Paul Tillich once asked, "If one is not able to die, is one really able to live?"[42] Facing one's mortality and coming to realize that death is an integral part of life can free persons to live with purpose and meaning. There is freedom in accepting that nothing, including death, "will be able to separate us from the love of God in Christ Jesus our Lord" (Romans 8:38–39).

Coming to that acceptance is not an easy thing for many persons. Hearing it does not necessarily make it real. Many older persons may hesitate to raise the doubts and questions that plague them because they have been led to believe that questioning reveals a lack of faith and is, therefore, something religious persons should not do. In addition, being afraid has been portrayed by religious institutions and culture alike as a sign of weakness.

Elizabeth Kubler-Ross in her earlier writings[43] identified a process made up of five stages which she found dying and grieving persons experience. Those stages, now widely known, include 1) denial, 2) anger, 3) bargaining, 4) depression, and 5) acceptance.

As we shall see, this process, understood as a typical description of a fluid and individualized experience, can help us understand what persons who experience smaller deaths (e.g. divorce, loss of home, widowhood, institutionalization) go through as well as what dying persons experience.

This was made clear to me a number of years ago when I was teaching a death and dying class at a nursing home. An eighty-four year old woman spoke up when I finished outlining Kubler-Ross' five stages and said, "Of course! I watch people who come to the nursing home (where she had been a resident for seven years) go through those stages often. First they say they're just in for the winter because their children worry about them on the farm, but they are going home in the spring (denial). Then they're mad about everything—the food's not good and the meals are at the wrong times and the night aides pick on them (anger). Next, they act real nice to the activities director and say something like, 'If you'll just let me have breakfast in my room . . . ' (bargaining). Then they get quieter but they don't want to do anything (depression). Finally, some of them, like me, decide that this isn't such a bad place and we make it our home (acceptance)."

Persons who are experiencing grief need understanding and acceptance. They need a place where they can vent their anger and their questions without guilt or fear of rejection. They need to know that others feel like they do and that whatever one's feelings are, they are okay.

When I agreed to teach that death and dying class in a nursing home (the class was composed of eight residents, five staff members, and three persons from the community), I became very aware of the fact that persons who are old in the 1980s grew up in a culture where death was a taboo topic. One mentally alert woman who was confined to a wheelchair said, "This is the first time I've ever felt I could talk about death in my whole life." She had plenty on her mind, and we were all stimulated by her questions and her thoughts.

One of the very practical things that resulted from that class was the establishment of a policy to hold a memorial service for residents who died in the chapel of the nursing home (in addition to the funeral which most residents could not attend). It became clear that down-playing death was not seen as a positive step by the persons in that class. "Death is a part of life, and we want to acknowledge the deaths of our friends and say, 'goodbye.'"

I could not help but believe that such acceptance and celebration of life and death is ever so much healthier than hearing it whispered through the corridors after the body has been whisked surreptitiously out the back door.[44] Death is a passage that can be prepared for and celebrated. Faith communities ought to take the lead in enabling persons to both prepare and celebrate.

One way to help persons prepare for death (ideally, before death is imminent) is to hold classes and forums where help with practical matters like wills and other personal affairs that need to be dealt with are discussed. Issues like donating organs and/or one's body and funeral practices can also be explored.

Persons who are dying and their families may need help with 1) financial concerns, 2) concerns of one's own and one's loved ones regarding personal loss, 3) arranging for medical care and other practical needs as a result of one's illness, 4) how to set priorities and make wise use of one's time, energy, and financial resources, and 5) how to handle psychosocial problems resulting from one's fears (e.g., pain, dying, loss of independence, loss of control of one's life).[45]

The ritual life of one's faith community can be studied and even transformed to reflect the meaning of the passage one makes through death.[46] Celebration of death and new life can be life enhancing and life transforming.

Because faith communities focus on what it means to be free and to be whole, they are in a position to help persons explore these issues. Because faith communities find their power and their answers beyond human power and achievement, they can speak to persons who are coming to terms with "the fact of limitation as well as with that of creativity, with the contracting as well as the expanding dimensions of life, with loss as well as with gain, with frustration as well as fulfillment."[47]

3) Divorce

Divorce is not reserved for the young and middle-aged. It creates additional problems for persons who divorce in old age because they grew up in a world where the cultural stigma attached to divorce was very great.

Between 2 and 3 percent of all persons aged sixty-five and over are divorced and over 10,000 persons in that cohort become divorced annually.[48] This should not be surprising since older couples may face failing health, decreased income, a need to readjust family roles due to retirement and/or health problems of one or both spouses, and perhaps reduced sexual expression.

Divorce represents the death of a relationship. It can cause immense pain and often lowers one's self-esteem. Clearly, divorce requires life reconstruction at a time when older persons may be over-taxed from dealing with multiple losses.

Faith communities, preferably on a cooperative and ecumenical basis, need to reach out to older persons who are divorced; this is especially critical because it is at a time when those persons are likely to withdraw from the faith community because they may feel unwanted and worthless.

4) Widowhood

Another neglected rite of passage is widowhood. It is true that the death of one's spouse is mourned and celebrated.

Nevertheless, there is often little help for persons who must reconstruct their lives without a husband or wife. Widow-to-Widow programs and other peer support groups may ease the pain such passages may cause.

Widowhood may be somewhat easier to cope with than divorce since it does not carry a cultural stigma. Neverthe-less, it is often a stressful time because one has lost one's most important significant other. Women are much more apt to be widowed than men[49]; they may also have lost a significant amount of their income.[50] Both men and wom-en lose a socially acceptable sexual partner when their spouse dies and many of the couple's social relationships are either altered or severed.

It is important to recognize that since neither all persons nor all marriages are the same, how persons react to widow-hood will vary greatly. Persons whose lives centered in the family and marriage will respond differently from persons who lived a "sex-segregated life" where the husband's life centered on work and lodge, and the wife's life focused on the children, housewife neighbors like herself, and wom-en's work in the church.[51]

Faith communities should create an accepting and open atmosphere with knowledgeable counselors and teachers, and with resources that deal with all aspects of aging. Wid-ows should feel free to explore their guilt, fears, and hopes. Discussion of sexual issues including cohabitation and re-marriage should be encouraged if persons have questions and concerns (never assume they do not!).

Support and self-help groups for older widows have been found to be very beneficial. Some of these women may have lived in the shadow of their husbands, and they may suddenly discover that they have no identity of their own. Faith communities can encourage and assist them in developing coping skills and in becoming a person in their own right.

5) Institutionalization

Approximately 5 percent of the population aged sixty-five and over reside in an institution at any given time. However, 25 percent will spend some time in a nursing home.[52]

A profile of the one million older adults who reside in nursing homes in the United States indicates that their average age is eighty-two. Two-thirds are women, and 90 percent are single or widowed. Half have no close relatives, and all but 4 percent are white. Less than half are ambulatory, and 60 percent never have a visitor. Only 20 percent will return to their homes, and most will die in the nursing home after an average stay of 2.4 years.[53] Of course, we know that a few persons spend many years in a nursing home while many die within six months.

Faith communities can assist persons who are facing the possibility of needing to enter a nursing home. Helping persons explore options and then make decisions can be an expression of nurture and care. Classes for adult children and their aging parents who may need to consider institutionalization can provide both support and information.

Churches and synagogues also have responsibilities toward persons who reside in nursing homes. It is not enough to supply cookies one month out of the year and to lead a vespers service every six months.

Visiting and relating to that 60 percent who never have a visitor on a sustained one-to-one basis is a vital and concrete way to see that the widows are not neglected (see Acts 6:1) and the poor in spirit receive blessings (see Matthew 6:3).

In addition to ministering to the frail-old on a one-to-one

basis, persons of faith and faith communities have a responsibility to advocate for quality care that builds self-esteem and fosters a sense of human dignity.[54]

Taking religious education opportunities to persons who cannot go to where the opportunities normally are is another avenue of ministry. My own experiences teaching in a nursing home and interviewing persons who were enrolled in classes taught by others suggests that providing opportunities that deal with topics of interest to nursing home residents is a significant form of ministry.

Especially impressive was my observation of an "interview" with a woman whose alert mind was imprisoned when a stroke left her unable to speak. She never missed her class on world affairs, and she was stimulated by what went on. Sometimes she experienced great frustration because she had something to contribute and we were unable to understand. It would have been tragic to deprive her of learning opportunities and to avoid communicating with her because of our uncomfortableness with her inability to speak.

There are many forms which ministry to institutionalized persons can take.[55] It seems appropriate to provide the same caring ministry to one's members who are in nursing homes and to all persons desiring ministry in nursing homes in the community as is provided to one's own members. Though percentage-wise, their numbers may be small, their needs are great. And who is better equipped to listen and care when persons feel lonely and need compassion than persons committed to God, ministering through their faith community?

Life Transcendence

The suggestions that have been made thus far for a comprehensive, intentional ministry to older adults are somewhat overwhelming when one considers that we have yet to deal with what some consider to be the primary purpose of religion—namely, leading persons to salvation or saving souls.

It is clear that older persons struggle with questions of meaning and purpose in their lives—after their more basic and immediate needs have been satisfied. Faith communities are founded on belief in God and God's care and concern for persons. Each faith community makes basic theological assumptions which color the nature of that community and determine what and how it teaches.

Many of the persons I interviewed expressed "a need for spiritual help." One eighty-six-year-old woman with a college degree showed the interviewer ten fruit boxes filled with files holding underlined clippings and handwritten notes from classes she had taken in her church. There were files on topics like Genesis, Jesus' teachings, the prophets, and Revelation. Clearly, this woman had been a serious student of the Bible and of religion in general for her entire adult life. At the time of the interview she was a member of a weekly Bible study on Mark and of an adult church school class which was studying Leslie Weatherhead's *Christian Agnostic*. She found that book "really controversial," and she disagreed with much of it, but she was enjoying studying it nonetheless.

A man in his late sixties with an eighth-grade education said he participated in religious education classes because he "wanted to learn [about the] religious/spiritual part of life. Spiritual life is a mystery," he said.

Several older persons said that while they were confident about their faith and knew they had experienced God's presence, they felt inadequate about their ability to tell others about their faith. They hoped to gain that ability through religious education classes.

That many older persons who participate in religious education classes experience personal growth is illustrated by these comments. One man said, "Ask my wife! It makes me a more compassionate person." A woman observed that it gives her a "broader perspective on life" so she is "not as narrow-minded." Another believed making one "more aware of the needs of the world" is a "broadening experience."

While one man claimed church adult education is "sustaining" rather than "changing," a woman asserted that it "has to change you" because it "helps you grow in faith." A seventy-one-year-old widow pondered over this question of change for some time. "I've wondered about that," she said. "It doesn't hurt me. It's good for me. It's educational. You realize things you should be doing."

A seventy-four-year-old woman, twice widowed, said, "I hope it softens me in my attitude toward people. You learn to be open and to accept other people's ideas. The more we study, the more we open our minds."

1) Bible Study

There are many ways to engage in Bible study. Several of the methods which are often used lend themselves to a shared-praxis approach[56] in which persons bring their stories and visions into interaction with the community's Story and Vision as it is recorded in Scripture and as it is lived out.

A helpful discussion of varying attitudes toward biblical authority which examines Eastern Orthodox, Roman Catholic, fundamental Protestant, liberal Protestant, and mainline Protestant attitudes and beliefs about Scripture can be found in Randolph Crump Miller's book *The Theory of Christian Education Practice.*[57]

Bible study is not an end in and of itself; rather, it is a

means by which persons can come to understand God and God's Word for them. The task facing religious educators is to enable persons to "get inside the world of the Bible" and then to relate those insights as one seeks "at the same time to exist meaningfully in one's own secular world."[58]

Randolph Crump Miller divides the biblical story into five parts: "creation, covenant, Christ, church, and consummation." He maintains that these epochs call for commitment on the part of those who hear the word and respond.[59]

2) Exploring Issues of Concern

Religious education classes may choose to explore topics that are of special interest and concern. A wide variety of human, scriptural, printed, and media resources can be used to help adult learners focus on the questions they have.

There is no limit to the topics that may be explored. Topics like relationships between adult children and their aging parents, agnosticism, human sexuality, applying Scripture to life, dealing with loss, and the meaning of death and life have all led to lively discussions with classes of older adults.

3) Intergenerational Study

One of the rich opportunities for the entire faith community is intergenerational learning experiences. Finding ways for all ages to bring their varied life experiences and their questions, their care and concern for persons, and their recognition that their faith community is inclusive in nature is a challenge worth pursuing. There are a variety of resources available to assist those who want to learn more about intergenerational teaching-learning endeavors.[60]

Conclusion

We began this chapter with a poem by a rabbi, Abraham Heschel, that suggests that the old need ". . . a vision . . . a dream . . . [and]a sense of significant being." "Just to live is holy," he writes. Certainly, *to become* takes one along the road toward wholeness.

There are innumerable opportunities for religious education experiences that can enable older adults to become more whole. We have maintained that designing an intentional, comprehensive plan for ministry with older adults is what is needed.

That plan should reflect the insights we have gained from developmentalists, educators, and theologians. It should grow out of and reflect the nature of a given faith community.

One viable conceptual framework for designing one's plan is suggested by Elbert Cole and involves organizing services and educational opportunities around needs which older adults have for 1) life maintenance, 2) life enrichment, 3) life reconstruction, and 4) life transcendence.

Plans for ministry should always remain fluid and should be open to alteration and change as the needs of older adults change. Programs must never become the controlling factor. They are tools to be used to enable persons to live life with meaning—to free them to envision visions and dream dreams.

In this way, persons may experience the forgiveness and love of God. For Christians that may mean recognizing that "if any one is in Christ, he is a new creation; the old has passed away, behold, the new has come. All this is from God, who through Christ reconciled us to himself and gave us the ministry of reconciliation; that is, God was in Christ

reconciling the world to himself, not counting their trespasses against them and entrusting to us the message of
reconciliation" (2 Corinthians 5:17–19).

Chapter Six Notes

1. See Figure 3.4 and the discussion of Maslow's hierarchy in chapter three.

2. David O. Moberg, "Spiritual Well-Being: Background and Issues," *1971 White House Conference on Aging* (Washington, D.C.: White House Conference on Aging, February, 1971).

3. Ibid., p. 3.

4. Ibid.

5. Material for this section is based on a visit to The Shepherd's Center located at Central United Methodist Church in Kansas City, Missouri. I visited with Dr. Elbert C. Cole, founder, first executive director, and now executive committee board member. He graciously gave of his time and shared a wide range of newsletters and other publications with me.

6. Elbert C. Cole, "Lay Ministries with Older Adults," in *Ministry with the Aging: Designs, Challenges, Foundations,* ed. William M. Clements (San Francisco: Harper & Row, 1981), p. 257. Quoted with permission.

7. These ideas were included in an address Elbert C. Cole gave to a conference on "Human Values for Older Floridians" entitled "Strategy for the Community of Faith: Ministry to Older Adults."

8. Ibid.

9. Donald F. Clingan, *Aging Persons in the Community of Faith* (Indianapolis, Indiana: Indiana Commission on the Aging and Aged for The Institute on Religion and Aging, 1975), p. 11. Used with permission.

10. Refer to the discussion in chapter 5 on Maurice Monette's article, "Need Assessment: A Critique of Philosophical Assumptions" in *Adult Education,* Vol. XXIX, No. 2 (1979), pp. 83–95) in order to avoid a strict service orientation approach which fails to examine basic presuppositions.

11. Robert M. Gray and David O. Moberg, *The Church and the Older Person,* rev. ed. (Grand Rapids, Michigan: Eerdmans, 1977), pp. 164–167.

12. Cole, "Strategy for the Community of Faith."

13. For example, churches may be able to support a congregate meal program funded by Title III by providing the site.

14. Wesner Fallaw, *Church Education for Tomorrow* (Philadelphia: Westminster Press, 1960).

15. Oscar E. Feucht, *Everyone A Minister: A Guide to Churchmanship for Laity and Clergy* (St. Louis: Concordia, 1974) p. 149.

16. Mark Gibbs and Ralph T. Morton, *God's Frozen People: A Book for and about Christian Laymen* (Philadelphia: Westminster Press, 1964) p. 23.

17. See the following resources for help in recruiting training, and working with volunteers: Harriet H. Naylor, *Volunteers Today: Finding, Training and Working with Them* (Dryden, New York: Dryden Associates, 1973); Douglas W. Johnson, *The Care and Feeding of Volunteers* (Nashville, Tennessee: Abingdon Press, 1978); and Ivan H. Scheier, *People Approach: Nine New Strategies for Citizen Volunteer Involvement* (Boulder, Colorado: National Information Center on Volunteerism, 1977).

18. Feucht, *Everyone A Minister*, pp. 108–118.

19. Peter Berger and Thomas Luckmann, *The Social Construction of Reality* (Garden City, New York: Doubleday, 1966).

20. James R. Wood, *Leadership in Voluntary Organizations: The Controversy Over Social Action in Protestant Churches* (New Brunswick, New Jersey: Rutgers University Press, 1981).

21. Ibid., p. 85. While this study is dealing with how churches might transcend opposition toward social action on the part of church members, there is much here that could apply to motivating older volunteers toward leadership in areas and roles that are built on the basic value orientation of the faith community.

22. Clingan, *Aging Persons in the Community of Faith,* p. 20.

23. Older Volunteer Project, *Releasing the Potential of the Older Volunteer* (Los Angeles: Ethel Percy Andrus Gerontology Center, 1976), pp. 56–59.

24. Irene K. Ogawa, "Old Age Education: An Approach to Dealing with Aging and Retirement," *Religious Education,* Vol. 49 (September-October, 1974), p. 607.

25. *Brookside Manor* (needs of institutionalized elderly) Institute of Gerontology, Ann Arbor, Michigan: *End of the Line* (decline, frustration of aging and helping agency personnel) Institute of Higher Education, Research and Services, University of Alabama; *Simulating Sensory Losses* (simulates loss of sight, hearing, dexterity, etc.), Dr. Isao Horinouchi, School of Public Health, University of Hawaii; *Taking a Chance on the Later Years* (card game dramatizing losses), Institute of Gerontology, Ann Arbor, Michigan.

26. *Minnie Remembers* (5 min., 16mm, color), Mass Media; *Nobody Ever Died of Old Age* (16mm), Films Incorporated; *Peege* (28 min., 16mm, color), Phoenix; *Volunteer to Live* (16mm, documentary on the Shep-

herd's Center), TV Film Library, 475 Riverside Dr., New York, New York 10027; *The Wild Goose* (16 mm), Films Incorporated; *Close Harmony* (30 min., 16mm, color), Learning Corporation of America.

27. Resources might include Allen J. Moore, "The Family Relations of Older Persons," in *Ministry with the Aging*, ed. William Clements (San Francisco: Harper & Row, 1981), pp. 175–192; Muriel Oberleder, *Avoid the Aging Trap* (Washington, D.C.: Agropolis Books, 1982); Earl A. Grollman and Sharon H. Grollman, *Caring for Your Aged Parents* (Boston: Beacon Press, 1978); Ethel Shanas, "Social Myth as Hypothesis: The Case of the Family Relations of Old People," in *Aging and the Human Spirit* ed. Carol LeFevre and Perry LeFevre (Chicago: Exploration Press, 1981), pp. 128–134.

28. Elbert Cole, "Lay Ministries with Older Adults," in *Ministry with the Aging*, ed. William M. Clements (San Francisco: Harper & Row, 1981), pp. 257–258.

29. See Appendix C.1 for a listing of "15 Positive Tests for Action." This is a good beginning point for congregations that want to assess where they are and to move toward an intentional ministry with older adults. An excellent resource for congregations is Mark Bergmann and Elmer Otte, *Engaging the Aging in Ministry* (St. Louis: Concordia, 1981).

30. Following a law suit brought by residents of the Pacific Home (United Methodist), a great many important issues regarding the responsibility for and control of such institutions were raised. The Pacific Homes class-action suits (1977–1980) against the Pacific and Southwest Annual Conference of the United Methodist Church as well as several national church agencies and the United Methodist Church as a denomination were settled out of court. These suits raised both legal and moral consciousness on the part of denominations about their involvement with and responsibility for church-related institutions and ministries.

31. Clingan, *Aging Persons in the Community of Faith*, pp. 48–51.

32. Resources on adult day care include *Adult Day Care in the U.S.: A Comparative Study* (Washington, D.C.: Transcentury Corp., 1978); Jeanne G. Gilbert, "The Day Care Center: An Alternative to Institutionalization of the Elderly" in *Long Term Care and Health Services Administration Quarterly* (Spring, 1977); Philip G. Weiler and Eloise Rathbone-McCuan with other contributors, *Adult Day Care: Community Work with Elderly* (New York: Springer, 1978); Eloise Rathbone-McCuan and Martha Warfields, "Geriatric Day Care in Theory and Practice," *Social Work in Health Care*, Vol. 2., No. 2 (Winter, 1976–77); W. Weissert, "Adult Day-Care Programs in the United States: Current Research Projects and a Survey of 10 Centers," *Health of the Elderly*, Vol. 92, No. 1 (January-February, 1977).

33. Linda Jane Vogel, "How Older Adults Perceive and Legitimize their Adult Education Participation in Schools and Churches" (Ph.D. Thesis, Iowa City, Iowa: The University of Iowa, 1981). Other examples will be cited in this chapter simply by referring to the source in the text.

34. Moberg, "Spiritual Well-Being."

35. See Gray and Moberg for a more detailed discussion on "What Older Persons Can Do for the Church" (chapter 9).

36. Howard Y. McClusky, "The Adult as Learner," in *Management of the Urban Crisis,* ed. Stanley E. Seashore and Robert J. McNeill (New York: The Free Press, 1971), p. 438.

37. James A. Thorson and Thomas C. Cook, Jr., eds. "Preface," in *Spiritual Well-Being of the Elderly* (Springfield, Illinois: Charles C. Thomas Publishers, 1977), pp. xiii-xiv.

38. Maggie Kuhn, "The Church's Continuing Role with the Aging," in *Aging and the Human Spirit* ed. Carol LeFevre and Perry LeFevre (Chicago: Exploration Press, 1981), p. 239.

39. Kuhn, "The Church's Continuing Role with the Aging," p. 342.

40. Evelyn Eaton Whitehead and James D. Whitehead, "Retirement," in *Ministry with the Aging* ed. William M. Clements (San Francisco: Harper & Row, 1981), pp. 124–136.

41. Clingan, *Aging Persons in the Community of Faith,* pp. 34–35.

42. Paul Tillich, "The Eternal Now" in *The Meaning of Death,* ed. Herman Feifel (New York: McGraw-Hill, 1959), p. 32.

43. Elizabeth Kubler-Ross, *On Death and Dying* (New York: Macmillan, 1969) and *Death: The Final Stage of Growth* (Englewood Cliffs, New Jersey: Prentice-Hall, 1975).

44. Jaber F. Gubrium, *Living and Dying at Murray Manor* (New York: St. Martin's Press, 1975).

45. Richard A. Kalish, "Dying and Preparing for Death: A View of Families," in *New Meanings of Death,* ed. Herman Feifel (New York: McGraw-Hill, 1977), pp. 215–232; Also Richard Kalish, "The Dying Process" in *The Later Years: Social Applications of Gerontology* (Monterey, California: Brooks/Cole, 1977), pp. 174–182.

46. John H. Westerhoff III and Gwen K. Neville, *Learning Through Liturgy* (New York: Seabury Press, 1978).

47. Seward Hiltner, "A Theology of Aging," in *Aging and the Human Spirit,* ed. Carol LeFevre and Perry LeFevre (Chicago: Exploration Press, 1981), p. 54.

48. Lewis R. Aiken, *Later Life,* 2nd ed. (New York: Holt, Rinehart and Winston, 1978), pp. 152–153.

49. The U.S. Bureau of the Census reported that for persons 65–74 in 1978, 9.7% of the males and 41.2% of the females were widowed; for persons 75+, 23% of the males and 69.3% of the females were widowed.

(*Statistical Abstract of the United States: 1979*, 10th edition, Washington D.C.), p. 42.

50. Schaie and Geiwitz (1982) report that widows on the average have one-third the income they shared with their husbands. One-fourth of all widows sixty-five and over have incomes that fall below government-defined poverty guidelines (*Adult Development and Aging*, p. 196).

51. Ibid, pp. 195–199.

52. Aiken, *Later Life*, p. 65.

53. Ibid., p. 67. This profile was quoted by Aiken in *Parade* (July 17, 1977) p. 10.

54. Gray and Moberg, *The Church and the Older Person*, pp. 160–161.

55. For guidelines and concrete suggestions see Clingan, *Aging Persons in the Community of Faith*, pp. 42–45.

56. Thomas H. Groome, *Christian Religious Education* (San Francisco: Harper & Row, 1980), chapter 10.

57. Randolph Crump Miller, *The Theory of Christian Education Practice* (Birmingham, Alabama: Religious Education Press, 1980), chapter 5.

58. Ibid., p. 198.

59. Ibid., p. 199.

60. Dorothy Jean Furnish in *Exploring the Bible with Children* (Nashville, Tennessee: Abingdon Press, 1975) raises a critical question regarding intergenerational education when she asks, "Is it possible to provide a challenge for adults and children at the same time?" This question must be addressed whenever one plans intergenerational teaching-learning experiences.

CHAPTER SEVEN

Envisioning the Future

"I am Awesome Mystery
    which I will not profane or trivialize
Nor is anyone else
    to profane or trivialize.

Still to be Spirit!
    though dimly, and at times murky
Still to be lived moments
    which light up with significances!
    even though I am in process of disappearing.

Still to be a meaningful story
    since soon that will be all.

I have a story
    and I have a song
And the song will be sung
    till my day is done."

(Ross Snyder in *Aging and the Human Spirit*)

Nothing stands still. We are a part of a pluralistic society in a pluralistic and rapidly changing world. Alvin Toffler has suggested that a new future is emerging. It follows the agricultural revolution which was the First Wave and the industrial revolution which was the Second Wave. Now, he claims, a Third Wave is engulfing us.

This Third Wave brings a whole new set of ground rules for living. The old social institutions (e.g., family, church, and school) are becoming less important and persons are faced with greater flexibility and more personalized life patterns. This Third Wave is fed by deep psychological, economic, and technical forces which foster autonomy rather than consensus and cultural diversity rather than standardization.[1]

Whether or not Alvin Toffler is right in all of his predictions for the future, it is becoming increasingly apparent that tomorrow's world will be very different from the world of today. Generalizations that are made about older adults today will certainly not apply to older adults in 2000.

We know, for instance, that the discrepancy in the educational level between young and old is diminishing. Tomorrow's older adults will have more formal education on the average than persons who are now sixty-five and over. It is likely to follow, then, that they will be financially better off. That may mean that they will be in better health. Certainly, they will be more assertive and less willing to accept the word of persons in authority.[2]

Cynthia Wedel[3] has asserted that the rugged individualism and competitiveness that may have been appropriate for a young and developing nation are not appropriate as we move into our third century as a nation. Rather, a global consciousness in which cooperation and justice must be seen as integrally related to freedom is required. She suggests that theology, along with modern technology and psychology, can provide us with the tools that are needed to enable persons to grow and mature into the world and our culture, as they must, if they are to survive.

Adult Education: A Global Concern[4]

Adult education is "an integral part of lifelong education." It is necessary to foster "the full development of the human personality"; in today's world, that must be viewed globally.

UNESCO defines "adult education" as "the entire body of organized educational processes . . . whereby . . . adults . . . develop their abilities, enrich their knowledge, improve their technical or professional qualifications or turn them in a new direction and bring about changes in their attitudes or behavior in the twofold perspective of full personal development and participation in balanced and independent social, economic, and cultural development."[5]

One of the aims of adult education is to enable persons to develop the "aptitude for learning to learn." That becomes increasingly important in a world where the knowledge explosion is so great that no one can hope to know everything they need to know.

"Learning to learn" involves "developing independent and critical judgment" as persons develop skills in decision making. Methods should be flexible and should recognize that adults are able "to assume responsibility for their own learning."

There are "no theoretical boundaries" to appropriate content for adult education. It should address specific needs which will foster the development of community life and individual self-fulfillment. It should "cover all aspects of life and all fields of knowledge" for "all people whatever their level of achievement."

Christian Religious Education for the Future

Thomas Groome has suggested that Christian religious educators are called to deal with two basic questions: "Who are we dealing with?" and "How do we perceive our own self-concept in the event of Christian religious education?"[6] We have looked extensively at who older adult learners are. We have suggested that all persons who choose to share their faith through teaching should examine who they are and should be clear about the theological and educational assumptions they make. Then they may plan activities that help persons focus on the transcendent aspects of life.

Christian religious education for the future should be deeply rooted in the perspectives of one's faith community. It should be aware of and enter into dialogue with persons who live and act in the world around them. It should reflect a global consciousness regarding the pains and needs and dreams of all persons and communities.

Christian religious education for the future should be informed by the knowledge and insight of the social sciences. It should take cognizance of the developmentalists and those who seek liberation. It should also remain open to revelation—that is, to God confronting persons and revealing Godself to them in order that they might be redeemed.[7]

Christian religious education is meant to guide persons into faith-living. For example, Christian living can be viewed as a comprehensive term that incorporates one's religious beliefs, one's religious practices, one's religious feeling, one's religious knowledge, and the religious effects that result.[8] It does this by helping them make connections between the Christian Story and Vision and their own life experiences. It enables older adults to integrate past, present, and future as they feel, think, will, and act within the context of their faith community.[9]

Christian religious education seeks to move beyond transmission by recognizing the worth of every person and their ability to make responsible choices. It witnesses to God's acts in history, and then encourages persons to see and hear and then to reflect critically on what one has seen and heard. Persons are encouraged to relate their own life experiences to the experiences claimed by the faith community. Whenever the freedom to think critically about what is proclaimed is diminished, religious education runs the risk of not moving beyond religious indoctrination; thus, it might transmit the faith without opening up the learner to the possibility of transformation.

Christian religious education, if it is to enable persons to become more whole, should

Affirm the worth of every person,
  Accept persons as they are,
    Love the unlovable,
      Offer forgiveness which makes persons new.
Proclaim release, justice, and peace
  so that persons will respond by
    doing justice.
      loving mercy, and
        walking humbly with God.

Christian religious education enables persons to be pilgrims as they join others in faith communities on the road to becoming who they were created to be—loved and loving.

The Next Steps . . .

Christian religious education will need to speak to older persons in tomorrow's world in new and varied ways. Some of those ways are suggested below.

1) Christian religious educators will need to focus on questions of meaning rather than on answers to questions persons may or may not be asking.

2) Christian religious educators will need to acknowledge that truth can be found in many places and by using a wide variety of approaches.

3) Christian religious educators will need to know the persons who engage in the teaching-learning process—their pasts, their worlds, their dreams.

4) Christian religious educators will need to know themselves and the Story and Vision of their faith community.

5) Christian religious educators will need to have skills that enable dialogical interaction.

6) Christian religious educators will need to be pilgrims—on their own faith journey—learners who serve as guides to other learners on the pilgrimage that can lead everyone to knowing God and becoming whole.

7) Christian religious educators will need to work cooperatively and ecumenically to develop comprehensive, intentional ministry with older adults.

8) Christian religious educators will need to learn from and build on the rich experiences and resources which older adults bring to the teaching-learning process.

9) Christian religious educators will need to recognize the diverse needs and abilities of older persons—all of whom can grow and learn.

10) Christian religious educators are called to be open, authentic persons of faith who are willing to share their

doubts as well as their joys within the context of a community of faith.

11) Christian religious educators are called to be full participants in the life of their faith community—engaged in worshiping, witnessing, learning, and serving in the world.

12) Christian religious educators are called to be "becoming"!

Conclusion

My sister told me about a seventy-one-year-old woman who is greatly admired as a teacher in her church. I asked this woman to share her insights by responding to the question, "What is the most important thing for a teacher of older adults to do?" This is what she wrote to me.

"Get to know those you teach—all about them. Be interested in their family relationships. Are they happy and contented? Are they all Christians or are there those who need salvation?

"Keep in touch with them between class times. Pray for them.

"When they have specific problems, be available. Let them know you want to help.

"Don't emphasize the teacher-learner relationship. Rather, let them know you are their friend. Encourage them to contribute to the learning experience so that it is a time of real sharing.

"Be prepared to have your complete outline go out the window because of a question that was asked. Be patient—even if you only cover two verses in a whole period."

She concluded, "In teaching a Bible class to older adults,

I hope to accomplish a deep and abiding love for God in their hearts so that they will honor and trust God completely and so they will eagerly seek the answers for life's questions from God's Word daily. I hope they will come to see that every word is inspired and true and has the power, through the Holy Spirit, to change lives."[10]

It becomes increasingly clear to me that the faith community we make our own and the theological assumptions we make determine to a great degree both what and how we teach. This woman, though never trained as a professional religious educator, exemplifies many of the qualities which religious educators need:

She seeks
    to know those who engage in religious education—
      their past,
        their present,
          their hope for the future
    to express her care for them—
      through listening to them,
        through being there to help in time of trouble,
          through intercessory prayer on their behalf.
    to be an enabler—
      by deemphasizing the teacher-learner relationship,
        by enabling them to engage in real sharing,
          by being accepting and patient with persons
          as they are.
    to be flexible—
      willing to throw one's lesson plan to the wind,
        willing to listen and guide the group in exploring
        any questions that are asked,
          willing to go slowly and to realize that persons
          are at different stages in life's faith pilgrimage.

This woman, whose wisdom developed from her love of God and her love for persons, knows what it means to become and to engage in religious education so that others may come to understand that God's gracious gift can enable them to receive power to become whole.

Chapter Seven Notes

1. Alvin Toffler, *The Third Wave* (New York: Morrow, 1980).

2. See Erdman Palmore, "The Future Status of the Aged" in *The Gerontologist,* Vol. 16, No. 4 (1976), pp. 297–302, for a discussion on projections about the future relative status of the elderly in health, income, occupation, and education.

3. Cynthia Wedel, "Growing Up Adult in America's Third Century," *Religious Education,* Vol. LXXII, No. 2 (1977), pp. 156–162.

4. This section is based on a UNESCO document entitled, "Recommendation on the Development of Adult Education" which was formulated by the General Conference of the United Nations Educational, Scientific, and Cultural Organization which met in Nairobi (October 26–November 30, 1976) at its nineteenth session.

5. Ibid., p. 2.

6. Thomas Groome, *Christian Religious Education* (San Francisco: Harper & Row, 1980), p. 261.

7. Lewis Sherrill, *The Gift of Power* (New York: Macmillan, 1961), pp. 65–79.

8. James Michael Lee, *The Shape of Religious Instruction: A Social Science Approach* (Birmingham, Alabama: Religious Education Press, 1971), pp. 10–13.

9. Mary Elizabeth Moore, *Education for Continuity and Change: A New Model for Christian Religious Education* (Nashville, Tennessee: Abingdon, 1983), pp. 121–146.

10. M.M. lives in Oregon where she teaches a Bible study class to older persons in her congregation.

APPENDIX A

Vogel Study Data

Vogel's Subjects

There were forty-four subjects in this study who resided in the rural midwest. Seven resided in a town of about 1,200, and twenty-nine resided in a county seat town of about 8,200. Eight resided on farms nearest to towns with populations of 8,200, 1,300, or 3,600. Seven of those living in towns resided in nursing homes. One of the seven participated in a class held in her church.

The subjects for this study were, in one sense, self-selected. Teachers of all adult education classes scheduled for twelve or more hours which were sponsored by a community college in conjunction with a public school system or by a small liberal arts college were asked to distribute and collect interview request forms from all students who were fifty-five and over.

Enrollment statistics for noncredit adult education classes did not ordinarily include age. However, the public school board of education paid the tuition for all persons from the district who were sixty or over, so that information was available. As nearly as could be determined from that information and from talking with the teachers, all persons fifty-five and over who were enrolled during the fall term, 1980, agreed to be interviewed with the exception of one man enrolled in a college sponsored woodworking class. His wife participated in the study, but he chose not to return the interview request form.

One class was offered at a nursing home facility in the community, and the six persons judged by the teacher and the activities director to be most alert and involved in that class agreed to be interviewed. Two persons over fifty-five were enrolled in regular college classes, and they also agreed to participate in this study.

Twenty-three persons fifty-five and over were enrolled in a school-sponsored class in a rural midwest county seat town in the fall term, 1980. Twenty-two of the twenty-three participants returned the interview request form, and they were interviewed.

Interview request forms were also given to teachers of classes sponsored by five Protestant churches. Twenty-two older adults from classes sponsored by five churches agreed to be interviewed. Two of the churches were United Methodist; the others included a Presbyterian United Church of Christ, a Baptist church, and an American Lutheran church.

Priests from two Roman Catholic churches were contacted, but their churches were not offering any adult education classes. This is a reflection of the fact that Roman Catholics in northwest Iowa do not have anything comparable to the Protestant Sunday School. The educational thrust in the Roman Catholic church in this area has been toward parochial schools for children and youth. This is illustrated by the fact that twenty-two parishes support four parochial high schools, with more than ten feeder schools.

It is important to note, however, that in the last few years the emphasis seems to be shifting toward community-based programs for all ages in many areas across the United States.

Thus, forty-four interviews were conducted between October 20, 1980, and January 17, 1981. Twenty-one persons were participating in a school-sponsored class; twenty-one persons were participating in a church-sponsored class; and two persons were participating in both a church and a school class. See Tables A.1 and A.2 in this Appendix for more data on the participants.

After all of the interviews were completed, age, sex, and education level of all persons fifty-five and over in eight of the church-sponsored classes from which participants came were collected to ascertain how representative of all church participants the church interviewees were. If a study were done of all older adult participants in these communities, the data suggest that the education level would not vary greatly between providers, but there would be more persons participating in church-sponsored classes than in school-sponsored classes.

Twenty-three of the forty-four subjects interviewed were between the ages of sixty and sixty-nine. The average age of school-sponsored participants was 69.4. If the six nursing home resident participants were excluded, the mean would be 64.8. The average age for church-sponsored participants was 69.2. The two groups were quite comparable. It is also noteworthy that the

Table A.1

Adult Education Classes Referred to in Vogel's Study

Church sponsored classes	Interviewees
Sunday School Classes	
Uniform Lessons: Matthew	6
Applying Scripture to Life (case method)	3
Advent	2
Galatians	2
Hymnal Study	1
The Christian Agnostic (Weatherhead)	1
Reformation	1
Exodus	1
Other Classes	
I Corinthians	7
Mark	2
Ten Commandments (Bethel Series)	2
Romans (Circle study)	1
Care and Witnessing (two year course)	1

Note: Seven persons were participating in two church classes at the time of this study. Two persons included here were also participating in a school sponsored class.

School sponsored class	Interviewees
College Credit Classes	
Oil Painting Techniques	1
Cultural Geography	1
Economics I	1
Adult Education Classes	
Woodworking	4
Doing Your Own Thing (Art)	3
Crocheting	3
Ballroom Dancing	2
Signing for the Deaf	2
Sewing with Knits	1
Adult Education in Nursing Home	
Current Events	6

Note: One person was enrolled in two school sponsored classes at the time of this study. One of the persons included here was also participating in a church class and another was participating in two church classes.

Table A.2
Interviewees by Age, Education and Provider*

Church-sponsored education	Age					
	55–59	60–64	65–69	70–74	75–79	80+
Less than 8th						
8th grade grad			25	33		
Some high school					31	
H.S. grad		32	2,21	36		
Some college	37	27,39	35	26,38		30
College grad		24	28		29,34	5
Some grad school	40					7
Grad degree	3	1				

School-sponsored education	Age					
	55–59	60–64	65–69	70–74	75–79	80+
Less than 8th						12
8th grade grad		13,20,23		33	14	18,19
Some high school					15	
H.S. grad	43		41	6		
Some college	4	17	11,42,44	9		
College grad		22	16,28			
Some grad school						
Grad degree		10	8			

*The numbers are code numbers assigned to the interviewees in this study. Subjects 28 and 33 were currently enrolled in classes offered by both providers.

male/female ratio of the subjects in this study is quite similar to national statistics for older adult education participants.

Of those subjects having children, the school-sponsored participants averaged 3.3 children while the church-sponsored participants averaged 2.5 children. All of the subjects interviewed were church members, and all but one participant in a school-sponsored class attended worship weekly. She attended "spasmodically." One person each from the two groups was currently enrolled in both a school-sponsored and a church-sponsored class.

Six persons were participating in two church-sponsored classes at the time of this study. One person was enrolled in both a church- and a school-sponsored class while another person was participating in two church-sponsored classes and one school-sponsored class.

APPENDIX B

Becoming Intentional: Ministry with Older Adults

APPENDIX B

Fifteen Positive Tests for Action

Tests Over Which Congregations Have Control as They Plan for Ministry To, For, and With the Aging

Reprinted from the *NBA Memo to Congregations* published by the Department of Services to Congregations, The National Benevolent Association of the Christian Church (Disciples of Christ)

Donald F. Clingan,
Executive Director

The Following "Positive Tests for Action" have been compiled from the thinking of Dr. David O. Moberg, Professor and Chairman of the Department of Sociology and Anthropology, Marquette University, Milwaukee, Wisconsin, and the writer of the background paper on "Spiritual Well Being" for the 1971 White House Conference on Aging; Ms. Margaret (Maggie) Kuhn, Convenor of the "Gray Panthers"; and Mr. Clingan, first President and first Executive Director of the National Interfaith Coalition on Aging.

1. **Loneliness.**   It has been found that elderly persons all over the United States are LONELY. What is the church doing about this very human factor?
2. **Architecture.**   Do churches plan their buildings and facilities keeping in mind the elderly?
3. **Finances.**   Do congregational budgets show a high priority in funds for ministering to, for, and with the elderly?

4. **Transportation.** One of the chief needs of the elderly is transportation . . . to the doctor, to the grocery store, to the pharmacy, to the church/synagogue.
5. **Accentuation on Youth.** Every congregation should accentuate youth, but not to the degree that the aging are forgotten.
6. **Timing of Services.** Do our congregations plan at least some of the services they provide at times convenient for the aging? Night meetings, for instance, are not the best for the elderly.
7. **Family Oriented Programing.** Do we remember single member families as we plan church fellowship and religious education events?
8. **Removal from Leadership Roles.** How often do we "shelve" our aging saying that younger people ought to have all the leadership roles in congregations?
9. **Loss of Respect and Dignity.** Have you heard some elderly person say in your congregation that he or she is "just retired?" What does this say to the dignity and respect they have in their congregation?
10. **Out of Sight—Out of Mind.** In our "fear of aging," do we try to put the aging who need us, the ill or lonely or poor, out of sight and out of mind?
11. **New Worship Styles.** How flexible are we in planning our congregational worship to meet all persons' needs and desires?
12. **Orientation to Social Action.** Some aging are social activists. Some are afraid of such action. Nearly all aging, though, do desire to be of some service to others if they are provided the opportunity in home repair programs, telephone reassurance, friendly visiting, etc. In what programs of service do you involve the aging in your congregation both in the planning stage and in the program itself?
13. **Retirement Policies, Pension Plans, and Benefits.** Have you had a hard look at your congregational retirement policies, pension plans, and benefits lately? Are they adequate for today and planned for the future?
14. **Democratic Planning for Elderly.** Do the elderly in your congregation, Home Center, and religious body as a whole,

have the opportunity to plan and direct programs for themselves?

15. **New Dimensions of Religious Education.** What programs of religious education from the kindergarten level through older adults are designed to prepare persons for the normality of the aging process and for the day of retirement? We are told that with the medical science we now know, people could live to be 120 to 150 years of age. At the same time we are envisioned to retire earlier and earlier even as early as 50 years of age. What will we do creatively in this world with 100 potential years of retirement?

Ask the above questions in your congregation. Are you facing them straightforwardly? They are "positive tests for action" over which you DO HAVE CONTROL!

(Donald F. Clingan, *Aging Persons in the Community of Faith*, pp. 55–56. Used with permission.)

Glossary

AGE COHORT: Those individuals who were born during the same general time period.

AGE GRADING: A process of assigning social roles and prestige to persons in relation to their age.

AGE NORMS: Social expectations of what is considered proper behavior at particular ages.

AGISM: Prejudice and discrimination directed toward people simply because they are old.

CHRISTIAN RELIGIOUS EDUCATION: Planned activities by members of a Christian faith community which focus on God's actions in the present, on the faith community's Story and Vision, and on how persons'own stories and visions interconnect with the Community's Story and Vision.

CROSS-SECTIONAL RESEARCH: Study of the characteristics of a broad segment of a given population at one point in time (e.g., young and old might be compared at a given point in time).

DEVELOPMENTAL TASKS: A concept first used by Robert Havighurst in the 1940s to depict tasks which confront persons at given periods in the life span; mastery of the task leads to happiness and facilitates success with later tasks; failure causes personal unhappiness, social disapproval, and handicaps for succeeding with later tasks.

DOUBLE-LOOP LEARNING: A model for learning that identifies values, assumptions, and beliefs being held and holds them up to be evaluated in order to enable persons to think critically about the existing paradigm, in addition to seeking to solve problems within the paradigm; this is in contrast to simply accepting the paradigm and seeking to solve problems within that structure (single-loop learning).

ELDERHOSTEL: A network of colleges and universities that offer special week-long, noncredit courses in a residential setting to older people.

FAITH: An act of assent and obedience of the whole person which involves the intellect, the emotions, and the will (Tillich).

FAITH COMMUNITY: A community that transcends itself and that expresses itself through worship and through serving others: it lives out its faith by acknowledging its historical tradition, owning its contemporary experience, and moving out into the future with hope.

FLUID INTELLIGENCE: The capacity for insight into complex relations between things; the determinants of this kind of intelligence are largely independent of cultural background.

FRAIL-ELDERLY: Older persons with severe physiological and psychological impairment who require assistance in activities of daily living.

INTELLIGENCE: The capacity to accurately perceive relationships between things, regardless of substance; to recognize and recall what has been perceived; to think logically and to plan.

LIFE EXPECTANCY: The average number of years of life that persons of a given age have remaining at a specified age.

LIFE PHASES: A term used to differentiate between broad periods in the life span which are characterized by certain developmental tasks and/or marker events.

Life Stages: A term used to delineate periods in the life span; often viewed as hierarchical, sequential and invariant (e.g., childhood, adolescence, adulthood, old age).

Longevity: The average number of years lived by the members of a group.

Longitudinal Research: Study of the same person or population over a period of time (e.g., one group of persons might be studied over a twenty-year period to examine how they change as they age).

Norms: Standards or rules for behavior.

Old-Old: Persons seventy-five years of age and older (see young-old).

Personality: The ways of thinking, feeling, and acting that differentiate one individual from another.

Psychological Age: The adaptive capacities of individuals or the extent to which individuals can adapt to changing environment demands in comparison with the average.

Religious Education: Planned activities which focus on the transcendent aspects of life so that persons might explore and examine their relationship to an ultimate "ground of being."

Rites of Passage: Ceremonies or rituals that mark the occasion when an individual moves from one role to another.

Role: The expected behavior of one who holds a certain status.

Self: The sum total of everything that makes an individual unique—body, intellect, values, attitudes, and feelings.

Self-Concept: A mental blueprint of who one is; an individual's subjective evaluation of who one is, including one's body, behavior, and how one thinks and feels.

Self-Esteem: A sense of personal worth and competence which leads to self-confidence; a subjective quality formed, in part, from responses persons receive from others in the form of respect and assurance.

SELF-IDEAL: A mental blueprint of who one wishes they were like and could be.

SOCIALIZATION: A lifelong process through which individuals learn and internalize the culture and social roles of their society.

STORY AND VISION: Terms used by Groome to refer to "the whole faith tradition" of a community of faith. "Story" is the community's expression and embodiment of its faith tradition while "*story*" refers to an individual's experience and understanding. "*Vision*" refers to the lived response which the Story calls forth and the hope it embodies for the faith community (Kingdom of God for the Christian community) while "*vision*" refers to an individual's response and hope.

THEOLOGIZING: The study of and reflection upon one's faith as it relates to all of life. It draws on the history of one's faith community, one's present experiences, and one's hope for God's future.

VISION: See Story and Vision.

YOUNG-OLD: Persons fifty-five to seventy-four years of age.

Index of Authors

Index of Subjects